MW00889297

MOUNTAIN BIKING
ESSENTIALS

By Jim Bernstein

10 9 8 7 6 5 4 3 2 1

Contents

Introduction

Over the last ten years or so mountain biking has seen a huge growth among many people of all ages, and is continuing to gain in popularity for people looking to get outside and have some fun while getting in a great workout. With this growth in popularity comes the building of new trails and bike parks as well as bike related festivals, races, and other events.

Also with this growth comes the increased number of mountain bike brands, models, and components, and it can be enough to make your head spin! But don't let all this cool new technology scare you away from getting into mountain biking. You don't need to be a mountain bike expert or have an oversize wallet to get into the sport. It's easy to get yourself started with the basic equipment and then work your way up to the higher end bikes and components once you decide if mountain biking is right for you.

The goal of this book is to get you acquainted with what it takes to get into mountain biking when it comes to bikes, components, and all the other gear that goes with it. I will also be discussing things like proper bike maintenance and upgrades, plus I will get into riding techniques to help you get dirty out on the trail without having to be an expert.

I have been mountain biking for over 20 years and am still looking for ways to improve my skills and tune my bikes so they perform at their best. I also run a mountain bike website (**mtbcommunity.com**) where we do trail reviews, product reviews, videos, and a regular blog. With all the latest and greatest technology that is coming out on a regular basis, it can be intimidating to keep up, but as long as you have the gear that you need and are having fun then that's all that matters. So, on that note, let's hit the trails!

Chapter 1 – Why You Should Mountain Bike

There are many reasons why you should mountain bike, and once you get into it you will ask yourself how you ever lived without it. Many people will get addicted to it once they get out there and experience all the wonderful trails and nice people they will meet once they start riding. You might even get to the point where it's a huge part of your life and all you want to do... kind of like me! In this chapter, I will go over some of the many reasons you need to get yourself a mountain bike and hit the trails.

To Have Fun
The main reason you should ride mountain bikes is (obviously) for fun, and I hope you agree with me on this! If you are totally new to mountain biking or even bike riding in general, then sure there will be a period where you will need to get used to it and there will probably be some crashes coming your way, but that's just part of the fun!

Once you get comfortable on a mountain bike then that's when the fun really begins. If you are afraid you are going to crash, then guess what? You are most likely going to crash. There is a mental aspect to mountain biking that will affect how much fun you have and how much crashing you will do. When you see those guys doing huge jumps on TV or YouTube you might think that they have been training for years and you will never be able to do it. But, in reality, it's just that they have the confidence and guts to take on those kinds of crazy things and actually enjoy doing them rather than thinking of what can happen if it all goes wrong. Once you take on a challenge like a jump or steep trail and successfully complete it, most of the time you realize that it was much easier than you thought it would be.

Once you get your skill level up you will find yourself on YouTube constantly looking for videos of new trails that you can try out. (By the way, trailforks.com is a great resource to find local trails in your area, and they also have videos, pictures, trail conditions, and maps.) Eventually, you will find yourself branching out to other areas to check out some new trails and even find yourself looking for more challenging trails.

So, even if you find that you are having difficulty riding or not having the fun you think you should be having right away, then give it some time, because just like with most things, the better you get at it, the more fun it becomes.

For Exercise
Another reason to mountain bike is for the great cardio workout you get from riding up hills and even going downhill. Plus, you also work things like your legs, arms, and core while riding. The

Department of Health and Human Services recommends that you get at least 150 minutes of moderate aerobic activity or 75 minutes of vigorous aerobic activity a week. You can get that knocked out in one decent mountain bike ride. So, if you need to shed a few pounds, then why not have some fun at the same time?

Many times you will find yourself out for an hour or even two or three while riding, and even though you might not be moving the entire time, you will still get plenty of exercise. You can use apps such as Strava to track your actual moving time, elevation gain, and even calories burned (estimated). Once you start enjoying your rides then you will never want to (or need to) do cardio in the gym again. Plus, when you're having fun, it doesn't even seem like exercise.

When you are finished with your ride you can reward yourself with a nice meal (since you earned it), and once you get that much needed shower you will feel great. Plus, mountain biking is a great stress reliever and can take your mind off all of your problems.

To Socialize
One of my favorite parts of mountain biking is how you get to meet so many new people and end up with many more friends than you had before you started riding. Someone always seems to know someone else who rides, and then before you know it, you are riding with them as well.

Mountain biking is also a great thing to do with your friends just as a way to hang out and have some fun. And after a good ride, you can go out and have something to eat or maybe a beer and socialize even more. Plus it can make for great conversation while doing so, and if you are into bragging rights, then there is plenty of opportunity for that!

If you don't have any friends that like to ride then you can join a mountain biking group, where you should make some new friends rather quickly. These groups like to plan rides and often welcome other riders that want to tag along and ride new trails. If you like the people in the group, then all you need to do is join up and you have your riding friends after all. Many of these groups will hold social events outside of the usual rides as well.

Many bike shops also host group rides and welcome others to join them. If you like riding with a particular group of people on these rides, then you can become a regular as well. (If you are lucky, you can become friends with the owner and get yourself some discounts!) These groups usually have Facebook or Strava groups that you can join and be notified of the upcoming group rides. If you end up being a serious rider then you most likely will end up being a serious Strava user.

To Explore

With all the trails around the local mountains (assuming there are mountains where you live), it's hard to go check them all out on foot, and for the most part you can't take any motorized vehicles on these trails. This is where a mountain bike can come in handy.

If you have ever looked on a map site such as Google Maps and viewed the satellite mode, you might have noticed that there are trails all over the place. I often wonder how all of these trails got here when I have never seen anyone building them! Regardless, there are thousands of miles of trails to be explored and more are being created all of the time. Some of them might be short or not too exciting, but many of them will take you out into the wilderness with some great views of nature.

Mountain biking allows you to explore these trails faster than you could if you were to do it on foot and makes it a lot more fun at the same time. You can use an app such as the one from Trailforks and view your location in relation to the trails in real time, or if you use something like a Garmin (discussed later in this book) while riding, you can see the trail on your screen as you ride.

Once you explore all the trails in your area you will then know which ones your favorites are and then ride them over and over. And when you use an app like Strava, you will start tracking your performance and progress and strive to ride farther and faster. Then you can take your bike to new locations and discover some new and exciting trails that might be better than the ones you have at home.

Competition

If you are the type of person who is competitive and likes to be the best at everything you do, then mountain biking might be what you need to fulfill the need to win. Not only can you compete with your friends and see who can get up and down the hill faster, you can also enter races to see how you stack up against others.

There are many types of mountain bike races with a wide variety of classes. You can race in categories such as cross country, Enduro, downhill, gravel, and so on. Plus there are various skill levels, such as beginner, pro, and expert. Most of the time they take these skill levels and break them down even further into age categories.

You don't need to have any racing experience to enter a mountain bike race and can enter any category you desire. Just be warned that if you sign up for a skill level that you are overqualified for and keep on winning races, you will get bumped out of that category and have to enter into a more difficult one. Some people take these races very seriously while others do it just for the experience. Many times you will be racing with hundreds of other riders, so it can get quite exciting.

Chapter 2 - Categories of Mountain Bike Riding

Not all mountain biking is the same, and there are many different categories of riding styles, trails, and bike types. Most likely, you won't know which type of riding you will be doing right off the bat unless you have been watching Red Bull TV and YouTube and decided what style you want to ride based on what you have seen. Even if that is the case, you will not be a downhill racing champion right out of the gate without learning how to properly control your bike and take on the basic trails first.

If you have experience with biking (such as racing BMX as a kid or riding motorcycles), then you will have quite the advantage when starting mountain biking and will be able to more easily take on different types of riding styles and terrain. In this chapter, I will be discussing the main types (or categories) of mountain biking so you will know what each one entails and what it takes to get into that style of riding. Keep in mind that you are not limited to one type of riding. You can do everything if you like, assuming you have the appropriate type of bike for the task. Sure you can ride a steep downhill trail on your cross country bike, but it will probably be more scary than it is fun... and possibly painful!

When reading about each category of mountain biking, keep in mind that there are specific bikes for each type (which I will go over in Chapter 3). The trend lately is to make bikes that are good at multiple types of riding, so you don't have to buy yourself a bike for each type, because that can add up quickly. One other thing to keep in mind is that the area you live in and the trails you ride will help determine what category of riding you will be doing.

Cross Country (XC)
Cross country riding can be thought of as the type of riding you would do if you were looking for easier trails where you can cover longer distances without having to worry about things like super technical trails or steep downhills. Cross country trails can consist of singletrack or fire road trails and is a good place to start if you are new to mountain biking since it tends to be easier and safer than some of the other types of riding.

All Mountain\Trail
This type of riding consists of more rugged terrain and steeper, more challenging trails where you will need more skill to ride successfully. All Mountain used to be the term used to describe this kind of riding, and it made sense because it means you can take on all kinds of mountains and conditions. Lately, this term has been replaced with Trail, which I guess can be thought of as any kind of trail. (I prefer the term All Mountain myself!) Regardless of the term you wish to use, just

know that All Mountain\Trail is one of the most popular types of riding because you can ride some really exciting trails without having to be a mountain biking expert. Then again, if you don't have any challenging trails around where you live, then you might be doing more Cross Country riding or traveling to ride other trails.

Enduro

Enduro is the next step above All Mountain, and also refers to a category of racing. It's a combination of All Mountain and Downhill, where you will be taking on steep, technical terrain and also doing some climbing as well. Enduro is more of a style of riding than a type of trail, and people who prefer this riding style usually like taking more risks and challenging themselves by riding more difficult trails at higher speeds.

Downhill

Downhill riding is exactly how it sounds—riding downhill. Some people prefer only to ride downhill and not spend any time pedaling or putting in the work to get to the top of the hill. Many times you do downhill riding by taking a shuttle to the top of the mountain with your bike and then ride down. There are many local companies that will offer shuttle service (for a price) in areas that are known for their fun downhill trails. Downhill trails tend to be steeper, faster, and more technical, and the people who ride them do it for the speed and excitement level that you get from riding downhill at a high rate of speed.

Gravel\Cyclocross (CX)

Gravel and Cyclocross riding are not exactly the same thing, but are similar enough to put them into one category. They both take aspects of both road bikes and mountain bikes and combine them into one bike that can handle both types of riding. Of course, they aren't as good as a road bike on a road or as good as a mountain bike on a mountain, but these bikes can usually hold their own. Many people buy these types of bikes for competition purposes where they will do long distance races on the road and in the dirt.

Bike Park\Freeride

The last category of riding is one of the most fun types out there if you have the skill and the guts to do it. With the growing popularity of mountain biking, many ski resorts will transform their slopes into a mountain bike paradise (or bike park) in the summer when there is no snow. They will create fast trails with things like jumps, drops, rock gardens, obstacles, and other challenges. Then to get to the top, you take yourself and your bike on the ski lift and only have to worry about riding down. These bike parks usually provide maps with trail descriptions and difficulty ratings.

Freeriding is similar to riding in a bike park except you can do it without the bike park itself. Many people build bike park like runs out in the wilderness with all different levels of jumps, and then you are free to take them any way you like. If you get good enough, you can start doing tricks like 360s and backflips.

Trail Ratings

Now that I have gone over the different categories of mountain biking, I would like to take a minute and discuss trail ratings. These are something you need to pay attention to when riding new trails because if you don't, then you might end up getting hurt.

For the most part, there are four or five basic trail ratings, and they use colors to rate their difficulty levels. For these ratings, you will see green, blue, black diamond, double black diamond, and red or orange. Here is what you need to know about each of these trail ratings:

- **Green** – Green designates the easiest of trails and is suitable for beginners. They are usually not too steep or technical, and many times indicates an easy climb compared to something more difficult.

- **Blue** – This designates an intermediate trail and should only be ridden by riders with a decent amount of experience. Many times blue rated trails will have jumps or drops as well as rockier, more technical terrain. These are my favorite type of trails because if you're a good rider, you can usually fly down them without having to worry about running into something above your skill level.

- **Black Diamond** – When you come across a black diamond trail you should take your time the first time riding it to see what's in store for you. If you discover that you can handle everything on it or know how to avoid the things you can't, then you can take it a little faster the next time and not have to worry about any surprises.

- **Double Black Diamond** – When you see a double black diamond rating you should probably avoid it unless you have some advanced mountain biking skills. There tend to be things like bigger jumps and drops and there may or may not be a way around them. They also tend to be steeper and more technical.

- **Red or Orange (Diamond)** – Unless you are a professional rider you probably should avoid the red\orange expert trails because there is a good chance there will be something out of your skill level with no way around it. Riding these is a good way to hurt yourself.

Here is what these symbols usually look like on trail signs in North America. Other areas use slightly different designations. For example, European countries sometimes use blue for beginner rather than intermediate trails.

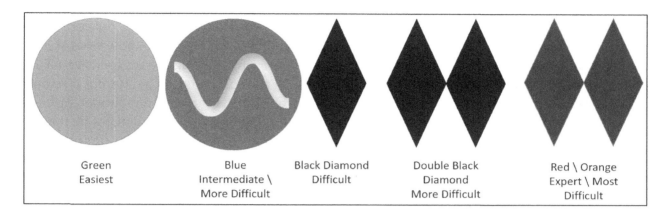

| Green
Easiest | Blue
Intermediate \ More Difficult | Black Diamond
Difficult | Double Black Diamond
More Difficult | Red \ Orange
Expert \ Most Difficult |

One important thing to keep in mind is that one person's version of a blue or black diamond trail may not apply to someone else. I've ridden black diamond trails that should have been rated blue, and blue trails that should have been rated black diamond (at least in my opinion).

Chapter 3 – Types of Mountain Bikes

Now that you have an idea about the different categories of mountain biking, it's time to get into the bikes that go along with these particular categories and then some. Once you figure out what style of riding is going to be your preferred type, then you can concentrate on getting the appropriate bike to go along with that riding style. Of course, you might not know what style of riding is going to be your favorite, so you might want to consider getting a less expensive bike to start out with so you don't have to worry about spending a lot of money on a different bike once you figure out what you really want. In Chapter 4, I will be discussing buying a mountain bike and go over the good and bad of buying a used bike. For your first bike, buying used might be the way to go so you don't break the bank before deciding if mountain biking is your thing or not.

Now that mountain biking has become so popular, there seem to be bikes made for every possible riding situation. No matter what type of riding you want to do, you will be able to find a bike that is made for it. Here is a listing of all the different types of bikes you have to choose from:

Cross Country (XC)
Cross country bikes are generally full suspension bikes, but they can also be hardtails as well. When I say full suspension that means there is a suspension fork in the front and also a shock in the rear. A hardtail will only have a suspension fork in the front. Hardtails will ride a little rougher on the rocky stuff but will climb better and will usually weigh less than full suspension bikes. One thing you should get used to when it comes to bike terminology is that the rear shock is called a shock and the front suspension fork is just called a fork, and not referred to as a shock even though it acts like one. (I will be going over suspension components in more detail in Chapter 8.)

Cross country bikes tend to be on the lighter side when it comes to weight than most of the other types of bikes. This makes it easier to climb hills because the more the bike weighs, the harder it is to pedal up a hill. The same goes for you and your weight. If you lost ten pounds you would definitely notice the difference when you were out on the trails. Frames for these types of bikes can be made from aluminum or carbon fiber.

The geometry of cross country bikes tends to be geared towards ease of climbing rather than downhill capabilities. There are many types of geometry settings to consider when manufacturers design these different types of bikes. One of the most noticeable is the head tube angle. This is the angle from horizontal to the angle that your fork sits at and is measured in degrees. The smaller the number, the more of an angle the fork will set at. Cross country bikes tend to have what they call *steep* head tube angles compared to other bikes, such as Enduro or downhill bikes, which will have more *slack* head tube angles. As you can see in the image below, the angle of the fork on the cross country bike is less than that of the Enduro bike. Also notice that the fork on the Enduro bike is longer, which is referred to as having more travel.

CROSS COUNTRY ENDURO

The suspension on cross country bikes is usually on the mild side, meaning it's not really designed to take on things like big jumps or drops and won't be as smooth on really rocky terrain. The suspension will generally have less travel, meaning how far the shock and fork can travel up and down to absorb the bumps. XC bikes typically have 100-130mm of travel in the front and rear.

These bikes will usually have narrower handlebars and skinnier tires, which helps out with weight and also rolling resistance. Usually, you will see tire widths around 1.9-2.25".

All Mountain\Trail
Trail bikes are the next level up from XC bikes when it comes to handling more difficult terrain and tend to be the most popular type of bike these days since they are very versatile. They tend

to be a little heavier thanks to their more aggressive setup and sturdier components. You can also get them with aluminum or carbon fiber frames, so going with the carbon is a way to take off the weight (even though it will take some weight off your wallet as well!).

The head tube angles will be a bit slacker as well, which makes it easier to go down steeper hills without feeling like you are going to go over the handlebars. Speaking of handlebars, they will also be wider, which helps keep you in control when things start getting out of control. Usually you will see handlebar widths around 760-800mm.

As for suspension, trail bikes will have more heavy duty forks and shocks with longer travel. Typically you will see the travel around 140-160mm. You might also find heavier duty brakes with four piston calipers rather than two, and larger brake rotors. Think of the disk brakes on mountain bikes working the same way they as do on your car or motorcycle. (I will be talking about brakes in more detail in Chapter 8.)

Trail bikes also use wider, knobbier tires for better handling and control over loose and rocky terrain. With those wider tires will come wider wheels that are designed to handle these more aggressive tires and are typically around 2.3-2.6".

Enduro

Think of an Enduro bike as a more aggressive trail bike that can do everything a trail bike can do, plus take on some more difficult terrain. Today's Enduro bikes are made to climb fairly well as well as go downhill fast. In fact, the line between trail bikes and Enduro bikes is begging to get blurred, and they might eventually become one category.

The biggest difference between an Enduro bike and a trail bike is that Enduro bikes have a more aggressive head tube angle for steeper descents and suspension with more travel, generally around 150-170mm. The suspension components tend to be more heavy duty as well.

You can get Enduro bikes with aluminum and carbon fiber frames, just like with the other bikes. They may or may not have wider handlebars and tires compared to trail bikes depending on the model. If you don't plan on hitting the gnarly stuff or doing Enduro racing, then you should probably stick with a trail bike.

Downhill

Downhill bikes are becoming a special niche type of bike since trail and Enduro bikes can now handle the type of terrain that was usually only attempted on a downhill bike. Now downhill bikes are most commonly used on only the most difficult of trails that are usually rated as black diamond or higher. They are also used for downhill racing, and if you have ever seen events like the Red Bull Rampage, you will see why they are needed.

When it comes to suspension, you will often see huge dual crown forks with 180-200mm of travel in the front with coil sprung shocks in the rear compared to air sprung shocks typically used on all other types of bikes. As you can see in the image below, a downhill bike is made to take on anything you can throw at it.

These bikes will also have wider tires (2.6-2.8") as well as wider handlebars (780-820mm), giving them greater control on the terrain that they were designed for.

Since these bikes are meant to ride downhill, they are very difficult to ride uphill. The gearing is much different than other types of bikes, plus they usually don't have as many gears to choose from. Also, you can't lock out the suspension for climbing, so when you pedal a downhill bike, you lose lots of your energy from bobbing up and down on the suspension.

Fat Tire

Next on the list, we have fat tire bikes. These bikes get their name from the size of the tire that they use, which is much wider than your average mountain bike tire, measuring in at 3.8 to 5 inches in width! With these wider tires, you can run much lower air pressure and use the tires kind of like shock absorbers to help cushion your ride.

Many people will use fat tire bikes in the sand or snow because they tend to float over these surfaces rather than sink into them like other types of bikes would do.

When it comes to suspension, you will find fat tire bikes with no suspension (rigid) and also in full suspension and hardtail configurations. Since the tires act as your suspension, many people go the no suspension route or the hardtail route. Some people say when you add suspension to a fat tire bike it's a bit overkill or counteractive. Below you will see an image of a fat tire bike with no front or rear suspension.

You generally don't see too many fat tire bikes on the trail, and to me, it's more of a novelty item than anything else unless you actually live someplace where you can use it for what it was meant to be used for.

E-Bike

One of the newest trends in mountain biking that is growing in popularity are e-bikes (electronic bikes) that help you ride by providing power from an electric motor via a battery stored within the frame. Where I ride, I tend to see a lot more of these bikes compared to even a year ago. And eventually there might be more e-bikes on the trail than regular bikes!

There are generally two types of e-bikes: the pedal assist type and the throttle type. Pedal assist is where the battery assists you only while you are pedaling. You can set the level as to how much assistance you would like, such as 10%, 30% and so on. The more assistance you use, the more battery it will use, therefore shortening your ride. As e-bikes advance, so do their batteries. The other type is throttle controlled and is sort of like having an electric motorcycle. You don't see these as much as pedal assist bikes. These bikes are usually limited speed-wise regarding how much the battery will help you. 20 mph is a typical cutoff speed for e-bikes.

E-bikes are banned from some areas, especially parks so if you have been considering one you might want to find out if you can even ride it on your local trials before taking the plunge. But every year, they are becoming more accepted and someday soon they will probably be allowed everywhere. One thing to keep in mind is that when the battery dies, you are stuck pedaling the bike on your own power. You might think this is not a problem, but e-bikes are much heavier than other bikes, making them more difficult to pedal. A typical cross country bike might weigh 26-30 lbs. while an e-bike can easily weigh over 50 lbs.

There are two main types of e-bikes you will find. The full power models with the larger battery and motor and then the "lighter" models with smaller batteries and motors. Usually, you can get a lighter model down to around 38-40 lbs. with a carbon fiber frame. They will still give you a nice assist but at the same time you will need to put in some effort as well. Whereas the full power bikes can seem like they are doing all the work for you. There are some new bikes coming out that are pushing the low 30s when it comes to their weight but they usually have lighter components such as shorter travel forks and shocks and smaller brake rotors.

The image above is of the Trek Rail full power e-bike while the image below is of the Specialized Turbo Levo SL lightweight e-bike.

Most e-bikes have at least 3 power levels that can be adjusted on the fly as you ride to give you more or less power. They will also have some type of display screen on the frame telling you what mode you are in and how much battery power you have left. These screens vary from model to model as you can see below.

As for cost, e-bikes are on the expensive side and usually start around $5,000 and can run as much as $15,000. Plus replacement batteries can run you well over $500. Some people will buy an extra battery and carry it in their backpack while riding to give them extra range. Some models offer a range extender battery that you can hold in your water bottle cage.

There are many situations when e-bikes make sense, and that is when they are used for people who are just getting into mountain biking and would like to go further than five miles before wanting to pass out! They are also good for older riders who can't handle longer rides, but want to stay in the sport, and also for people recovering from injuries.

If you are new to riding, out of shape, or have health issues that make it hard to exercise you might want to consider a full power bike. But if you are an experienced rider who wants to get a little help but still get a workout, then the lighter models might be for you. Plus the lighter models feel like a regular bike on the descents while the full power models sort of feel like a tank that you are just pointing in a straight line and plowing through the terrain.

Gravel\Cyclocross

This style of bike is one of the newer types out there and is not commonly seen on the trail, but rather used for racing or long distance riding where you will have dirt and pavement. Cyclocross bikes are more for racing and are a bit lighter with steeper head tube angles for sharper turning. They are more similar to road bikes than gravel bikes are.

Gravel bikes are usually a little bit heavier and are also sometimes referred to as adventure bikes because you can load them up with gear and take them on long rides.

Both of these types of bikes will generally have road bike-style handlebars and 29 inch wheels with skinny tires. These tires are not as skinny as road bike tires but are also nowhere near the size of mountain bike tires. They will have a slightly knobby tread pattern, so they will be able to handle ok in the dirt yet not be too restrictive on the road.

Dirt Jumper\Slopestyle

The final bike type I want to discuss is called a dirt jumper. These bikes are designed for taking jumps and riding pump tracks. They are kind of like a mix of a mountain bike and a BMX bike. Generally, they are hardtails because the rear suspension gets in the way by absorbing energy while pumping on pump tracks and jumps.

As you can see from the image, the seat is a lot lower than on a regular mountain bike to keep it out of your way while you are doing your thing. Also, the frame will be smaller and shorter, and it will also have a shorter wheelbase. For the most part, you are standing while riding a dirt jumper rather than sitting. They also have a shorter travel fork with a stiffer tune to keep you in control of the bike. Dirt jumpers also have fewer gears than a mountain bike because you really don't do any climbing on these types of bikes.

Another variation of a dirt jumper is called a slopestyle bike. It's the same type of bike but will have a rear shock because they are used for more difficult terrain like huge jumps where you will want a little shock absorption on your landings.

For the most part, the most commonly used bikes on the trail will be the cross country and trail bikes since they are the most versatile and can be ridden on the greatest variety of trails.

Chapter 4 – Buying a Mountain Bike

Now that you have an idea of what type of riding you might want to do and what type of bike you want to get (hopefully), now you can focus on buying the bike that is right for you at a price you can afford. Ten to fifteen years ago there were not nearly as many choices of brands and models of mountain bikes as there are today.

For the most part, you will be buying your mountain bike at a bike shop rather than online or at a box store such as Costco or Target. Sure, these places might sell mountain bikes, but they will usually be the bottom of the barrel cheap type that you definitely don't want any part of. Not all bike shops will sell the same brands either, so once you decide on the model you want, you will need to find a place that sells them. And yes, you can find name brand bikes online, but you really need to check them out in person first before making your decision. Plus, if you have any issues with your new bike, it's much easier to take it back to the shop to get things straightened out. And, of course, it's always a great idea to support your local bike shops!

Hard Tail vs. Full Suspension
One factor that will have a big impact on what bike you end up with will be whether you want a hardtail or full suspension mountain bike. As I mentioned in the last chapter, a hardtail bike will not have rear suspension, and only has a suspension fork in the front. If you are just planning on riding smooth trails or fire roads and doing a lot of climbing, or maybe even racing, then you might not need suspension in the rear, and can save yourself some money and some weight.

Keep in mind that if you *do* go the hardtail route that if you start getting into some more aggressive riding on rougher terrain, you might wish you went with a full suspension bike. Many people who can afford more than one bike will have both types, and just ride the one that is appropriate for the trail that day. I always find that the front suspension is much more noticeable since you feel it in your hands and arms when you don't have any compared to the rear, but when you don't have any in the rear you will still notice it for sure.

Wheel Size and Material
Back in the old days, we really only had one choice when it came to wheel size, and that was 26 inches in diameter. Now we have two choices for wheel sizes, and 26 inches is not one of them anymore. A while back, 29 inch wheels started appearing on the scene, and some of us didn't know if they would take off or not. It turns out that they did and are now the most popular wheel size out there for mountain biking. The advantage of 29 inch wheels (or 29ers, as they are

commonly called) is the ability to roll over things like rocks smoother than smaller wheels. They also offer better traction and more efficient acceleration.

For the people who didn't want to take the jump, the next size to come out was 27.5 inches, which is a compromise between 26 and 29 inch sizes. Today you will find 27.5 inch wheels on more aggressive style bikes such as Enduro and downhill bikes. The advantage of this size wheel lies in cornering ability since the smaller wheel sizes can take corners faster. They also have faster acceleration and, of course, weigh less than 29 inch wheels. You will also find bikes that have a 29" wheel up front and a 27" wheel in the rear. This is commonly called a mullet setup and it allows you to have the rolling over objects ability of the 29" wheel and the handling of the 27" wheel.

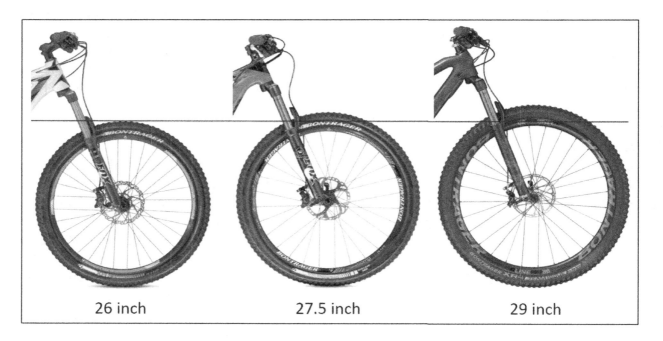

| 26 inch | 27.5 inch | 29 inch |

With the improvements in bike design, many manufacturers are able to make 29ers that handle and perform just as well as their 27.5 inch versions. Now you even see Enduro and downhill bikes with 29 inch wheels. (I have the feeling that the 27.5 inch wheel size might eventually suffer the same fate as the 26 inch wheel. I just hope they don't go any bigger!) One thing to keep in mind when choosing a wheel size is that if you are a shorter person, then you might want to stick with a 27.5 bike because the 29ers tend to be taller in size.

When it comes to what your wheels are made of, you have two choices, and they are aluminum and carbon fiber. Most new bikes will come with aluminum wheels unless it's a higher end bike that most likely has a carbon frame to go along with it.

Carbon fiber wheels will be lighter than aluminum wheels and are also stiffer (which is a good thing by the way). And just like with everything else in the mountain bike world, lighter is always more expensive. A nice set of carbon wheels can cost you $1,200 and up whereas you can get a nice set of aluminum wheels for $600 and up.

Some people will tell you that aluminum wheels are stronger and some will say carbon is stronger. It really comes down to how each type can get damaged. You can't bend a carbon wheel like you can an aluminum wheel, but you can crack them (but it's very hard to do so). Either way, you really need to put some effort into bending or cracking a nice set of wheels these days.

Aluminum vs. Carbon Fiber Frames

Just like with wheels, you have a choice between aluminum and carbon fiber frames. Once again, the carbon will be lighter, stiffer, and, of course, more expensive. When carbon frames first started appearing in the mountain biking world, they were more of a luxury and very expensive. With new frame manufacturing technology, now having a carbon fiber frame is not just for the rich anymore. Manufacturers actually have the process down to where they can make different types of carbon fiber frames at different thickness levels, which allows them to price them at different levels.

When you choose a model with a carbon frame, you usually get better components, such as a nicer drivetrain, wheels, brakes, and so on. One thing you will notice when shopping for a new bike is that one model may have several levels. For example, Trek will make something like their Remedy model in various "trim levels", such as the Fuel EX 7, Fuel EX 8, Fuel EX 9.8, and Fuel EX 9.9, with the 9.8 and 9.9 versions having partial carbon or full carbon frames. The higher the number after the bike name, the higher the price, because you get better components the higher up you go. This allows you to have some choices to keep things in your price range and get the components that work best for your budget.

I mentioned partial carbon and full carbon frames above. Some bikes will come with a carbon main frame while having an aluminum seat stay or chain stay to save on manufacturing costs and allow them to sell the bike cheaper. The seat stay and chain stay together are commonly called the rear triangle.

I recommend getting a bike with a carbon fiber frame if you can afford it because you would be amazed at how much difference a couple of pounds will make when it comes to the ease of climbing. If you end up with an aluminum frame, then there are other ways to lighten up your bike such as swapping out your aluminum handlebars, cranks, and wheels for carbon as you can afford to do so.

Suspension Choices

Suspension is one of the more important things to consider when buying a mountain bike because not all forks and shocks are the same. Once you decide what type of bike you are going to buy, that will determine what your suspension choices will be, since you can't just add whatever fork and shock you want to a bike unless you do a custom build. Even if you do go the custom build route, there are still limitations as to what suspension you can add to a particular frame.

For the most part, you will be using air sprung suspension rather than coil sprung suspension. In the old days, coil sprung suspension was much more common until they figured out a way to get the same level of shock absorption by using air. You will still see coils being used on Enduro and downhill bikes and mostly in the rear. I have always been a fan of coil suspension when it comes to taking on super rocky terrain.

When it comes to fork choices, you will usually be offered choices in travel length, stanchion size, and adjustability. I will be going over suspension in more detail in Chapter 6, but for now just know that your fork choices will be determined by the bike manufacturer and what model level you choose to go with. For the most part, the fork will look something like the Fox 36 or the RockShox SID in the image below on higher end bikes. Generally, the higher the level of the bike, the better the stanchions when it comes to their coating (If you were wondering what a *stanchion* is, it's the gold part of the fork as seen on the Fox 36). Going back to the Fox 36, the one in the image has their Kashima Coating, which is supposed to offer smoother movement and higher scratch resistance.

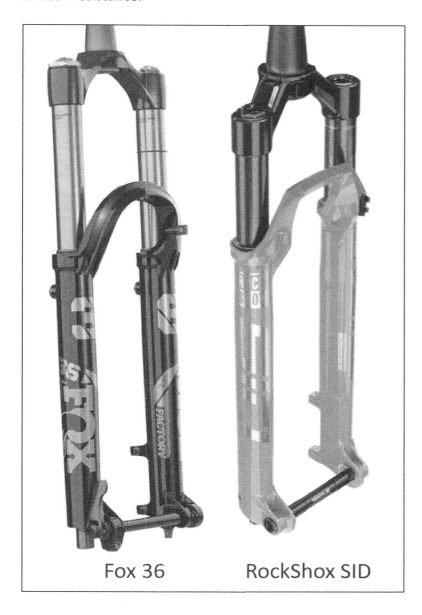

Fox 36   RockShox SID

For the shock choices, you might get some choices as to what adjustments come on the bike and whether it's air sprung or coil sprung. The same thing I mentioned about the special coatings also applies to shocks as well. Cross country bikes will usually have less aggressive shocks and always be air sprung, and many times on trail and Enduro bikes you will see larger shocks with extra air canisters on the side. This allows for more air volume, which helps on rougher terrain, and are often called piggyback shocks. Many downhill bikes will come with coil sprung shocks, which have been making a comeback lately.

Examples of rear shocks

New vs. Used
I mentioned in Chapter 1 how you might want to buy a used bike for your first bike to make sure that mountain biking is something you want to stick with for the long term. There are advantages and disadvantages to each option, and I will go over these differences next.

Buying New
- Never been used by anyone else.
- Having a warranty.
- If you have an issue, you can take it back to the bike shop.

- Many bike shops offer free tune-ups on the bikes they sell.
- More expensive than a used bike.
- You might not be able to afford the model you want if you buy it new.

Buying Used
- Cheaper than a used bike—usually by quite a bit.
- You can get a higher end model because it will be cheaper.
- Sometimes used bikes have been upgraded with higher end components.
- No warranty.
- You might not be able to see damaged components.
- Wear and tear from being ridden.
- You are on your own for tune-ups.
- Trusting strangers, to be honest.

If you decide you want to buy a new bike, then make sure you shop around and compare prices from various bike shops and online. I would definitely buy from a bike shop, but if you see a lower price online, they will most likely match it. Plus, you can usually wheel and deal on prices like you can when buying a car or get them to throw in some extras like a helmet and gloves. Try and stick with a bike shop that is close to you because if you have an issue or get the free tune-up deal, you don't want to have to drive a long distance each time you go back to the shop.

When it comes to buying a used bike, there are a couple of ways to go about it. You will most likely be doing this online, and you may have to take a chance on buying the bike sight unseen. If you use a site like Craigslist, then you can find bikes locally, but then again you never know what kind of people you will be dealing with on Craigslist. You can also use apps like Letgo and OfferUp to find bikes near you.

I like to use a site called **pinkbike.com** because it's one of the world's largest mountain bike sites, and they have a dedicated buy and sell classified section where you can find anything from complete bikes to pretty much every bike component you can think of. Since the people on the site are bikers and you have to create a profile to post things for sale, it's more trustworthy than Craigslist. You will need to create your own account to message people about the items they are selling.

Chapter 4 – Buying a Mountain Bike

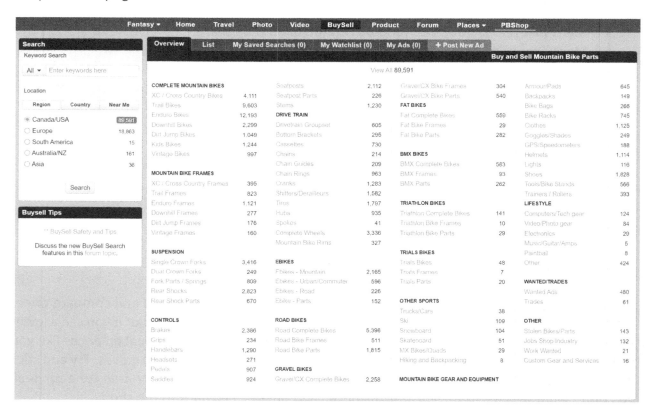

Once you are on there, you can select your region and then type in your search term or select from one of the categories on the right.

Then you can fine-tune your search by things such as year, wheel size, frame size, and so on. Most people will post multiple pictures of the bike they are selling as well as what components or upgrades come with the bike.

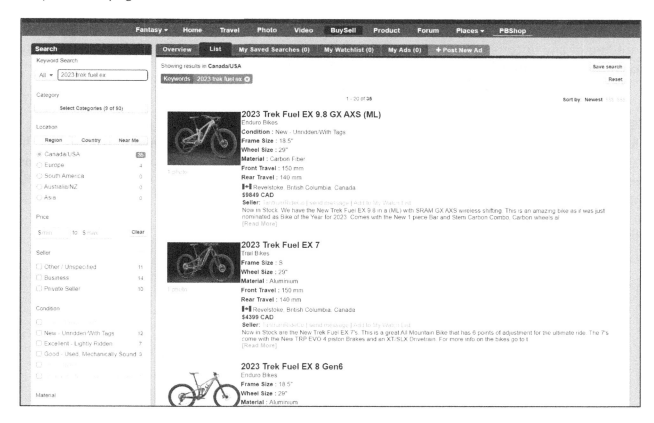

If you can't find something locally, then most of the time the seller can ship the bike to you for an additional cost. Keep in mind that this means partially disassembling the bike to fit it in a bike shipping box. Then you will have to reassemble it or have a bike shop do it for you. You might even be able to arrange to have the bike shipped to your local bike shop rather than your house.

Bike Demos

Many bike shops will have what they call "demo days", where they will let you come by and borrow a bike for an hour or so to let you try it out on some local trails. Sometimes the demos will be held at the bike shop itself, and other times they will be held at a local trail. All you need to do is bring your driver's license and a helmet etc. and they will fit you on the right size bike, adjust the suspension for your weight, and send you off on the trail.

The bike shops will often have many makes and models that they sell with the goal being to get you interested in one of their bikes to make a future sale. Depending on how many people show up, you can usually demo more than one model so you can see how each one actually feels on the trail.

If you are a Facebook user, then you might want to follow your local bike shops so you will be notified of any upcoming demo days. Or you can just call them and see when they are planning on having the next one.

Bike Sizing

Mountain bikes are not a one-size-fits-all type of product, and not every manufacturer uses the same methods to size their bikes. Some will use the small, medium, and extra-large designations, while others will use numbers like Trek, for example. They use a number system like shown in the image below, where a 19.5 is considered a large.

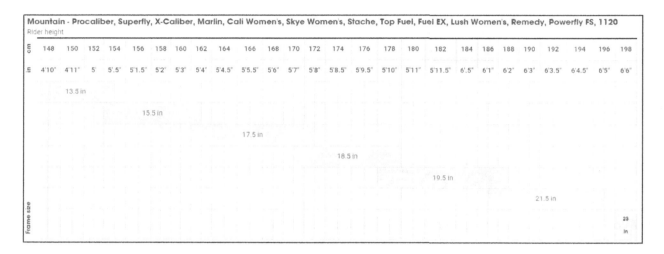

Since you might not know for sure what size you need or might be on the border of two different sizes, it's always a good idea to go "try one on" before making your purchase.

There are several things you want to consider when sizing yourself up for a mountain bike besides just the size:

- **Standover Height** – This is the distance between the top of the frame and your inseam when standing on the ground straddling the bike. You should have around two inches or so of clearance, and maybe a little more if you are a more aggressive rider. Just make sure to wear the shoes you will be riding with or something similar when looking at this measurement.

- **Reach\Stem Length** – This is the distance you have to reach the handlebars when sitting on the seat (saddle). Make sure you don't feel too stretched out or have your elbows too bent because that will take away from your bike control. This distance can be adjusted by replacing the stem with a longer or shorter one or changing its angle. The stem is what connects the handlebars to the bike\fork. You can also add spacers under the stem to raise the height of the handlebars.

As you can see in the image below, stems can come in various lengths and angles, allowing you to fine tune your reach. One thing to remember when it comes to stems is that longer stems generally help you climb steep hills better while shorter stems offer more control when going down steep hills.

Handlebars can also have a rise to them that is measured in degrees, which allows you to fine tune the way the cockpit feels.

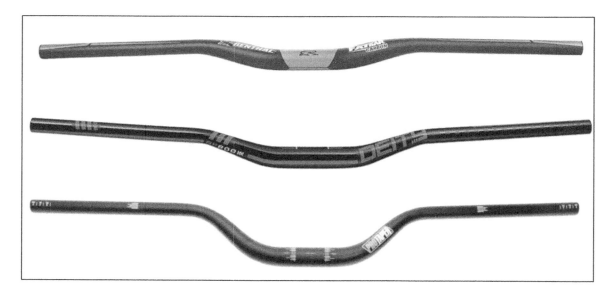

By fine tuning all of these components, you can really get a good fit between you and your bike when it comes to how you feel while in the saddle.

- **Seatpost Height** – The seatpost is what connects the seat to the frame, and the height of this component is very important to get right when sizing your bike. These days most bikes will have what they call dropper posts, which is a term to describe a seatpost that can be adjusted up and down on the fly. That way you can have it up for climbing and then drop it down to descend.

These seatposts come in sizes measured in millimeters, such as 125mm, 150mm, 170mm, and even 200mm and up. You can adjust the height as well by how far you slide them into the frame, allowing you to get the perfect riding height when the post is all the way up.

- **Seat Distance and Tilt** – When getting your bike configured, you will need to check the distance of the seat to the handlebars so that when you are sitting, you're in a comfortable position and on the right area of the seat. This can be adjusted by loosening the seat and sliding the seat on its rails backward or forwards to get the right position.

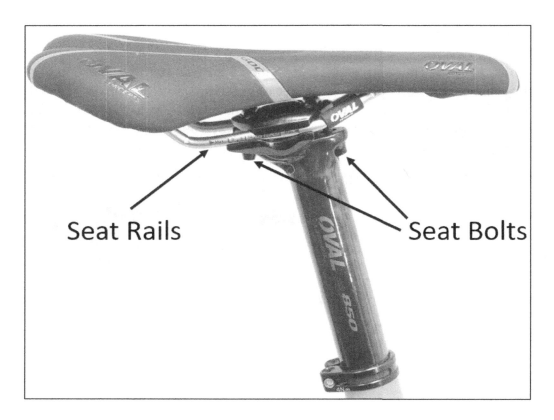

You can also adjust the seat tilt\angle up and down by making adjustments with both of the seat bolts. Most people like their seat level while others like it pointed down a little if they do a lot of climbing or pointed up a little for downhill riding.

- **Handlebar Width** – Choosing the right handlebar width is important because it will determine the overall feel and control of your bike when riding, especially on more aggressive and faster trails. The handlebar width is related to your stem length, bike geometry, and your riding style.

You will generally find narrower bars on cross country bikes and wider bars on Enduro and Downhill bikes. I would recommend starting with around 780mm if you are unsure where to begin. Most manufacturers will put the width of bars that they think go best with their bike, but that doesn't mean it will be best for you. If you *do* decide to change your handlebars, then start a little wider, because you can always cut them down if they are too wide. If you want to test to see if a wider bar is better for you, then you can slide your grips out a little to simulate wider handlebars. Just be sure not to ride your bike like this (except for maybe around the block to test it) because it's not a safe thing to do. You can also grip your bars more inward to simulate shorter handlebars.

Choosing a Bike Shop

Before you make your purchase, you should check out the local bike shops that sell the brands you are interested in. You want to find a shop that you can build a relationship with because you might be taking your bike back there for maintenance and repairs, so it's nice to get to know the people who work there. You might even get better pricing if you make friends with them!

But bike shops are not just for getting your bike fixed. Unless you are a strict online shopper, you will be in there all the time getting supplies and upgrades, so find one that stocks the things you need so you don't have to run around looking for these items. Plus, it's always better to support your local shop rather than buy online, even though you can usually find a better deal on the internet. Another thing to consider is whether the bike shop is geared more toward mountain biking or road biking. Many shops tend to favor one over the other when it comes to stocking bikes and parts and what kinds of bikes they work on.

The bottom line is that finding the right bike shop is like finding the right doctor. You want to make sure things get done right and you don't end up getting work done that your bike doesn't need. You also want to make sure you are not getting overcharged for labor or parts, so always get a quote for parts and labor when dropping off your bike and compare what they are charging for parts online to get an idea of if you are getting a fair deal or not. The same goes for buying parts and supplies. Doing your homework always helps... unlike in school.

Chapter 5 – Mountain Biking Accessories

Now that you have your shiny new mountain bike (hopefully), it's time to get ready to open your wallet and get all the things you need to go with it (and probably some things you don't as well!). Once you start getting into mountain biking, you will find yourself shopping for accessories to go along with it. Most of the items I will be discussing in this chapter you really do need, but there are also plenty of accessories you can buy that are more just for fun.

Clothing

I remember when I first started riding mountain bikes how I would pretty much wear the same clothes as I would for doing things like mowing the lawn or going to the movies because I didn't know any better and there weren't the choices available that there are now. When it comes to mountain biking, there are three main articles of clothing you need to think about. (Well four, actually, if you count shoes, but I will be talking about those next.)

- **Shorts** – For the most part you will be wearing shorts while you ride unless you are maybe riding somewhere super cold, but even then you can get yourself some slide on leg warmers to take care of that. Most mountain bikers go with the looser fitting shorts options, while others go with the tight spandex shorts like you see road bikers wearing.

  Most mountain bike shorts either have pads built in or come with a padded liner that fits tightly like the road bike shorts do. Then you wear the baggy shorts over top of them. The pads are meant for seat comfort to give you a little cushion since most mountain bike seats don't have a lot of padding.

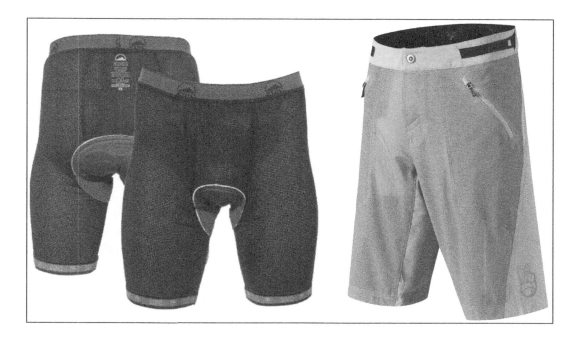

I always like to find shots that have zippered pockets for holding things like your phone or keys if you don't plan on wearing a backpack. If you have a favorite pair of shorts, you can always wear them over the padded liner rather than get dedicated mountain biking shorts. Just make sure they don't limit your range of motion when pedaling. Also, keep in mind that there are different materials used for mountain biking shorts. For example, downhill shorts are usually thicker and stiffer so they can take a crash without ripping.

You can also get padded shorts for crash protection that offer hip and tailbone protection to help cushion the blow when needed. These are typically worn underneath your baggy shorts.

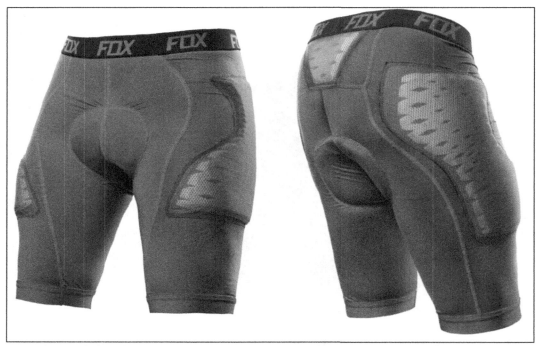

Most larger bike shops will have a decent selection of men's and women's shorts so you can see them in person and try them on to check their fit.

- **Shirts\Jerseys** – Wearing the right type of shirt (or jersey, as they are often called) is important when it comes to keeping yourself cool or warm depending on the weather you are riding in. Sure you can wear a typical cotton T-shirt, but when the weather is warm you will regret it because you will find yourself much hotter than you need to be and also soaking wet.

Biking jerseys are made from a special synthetic polyester blend designed to draw moisture away from your body to the outside of the shirt, where it can then evaporate more effectively. You will usually see these referred to as moisture-wicking shirts since they "wick" the moisture away from your body.

There are a couple of different styles of these bike jerseys. Some are loose fitting, like your average T-shirt, while others are more form fitting like you would see a road biker wearing. They can also have zippers in the front, allowing you to unzip them to get yourself some airflow when things get hot. Many will have pockets in the rear that you can use to store food and other small items. They will also come in short sleeve and long sleeve versions.

One thing I like to use is what they call *sleeves*, which is a slide on sleeve that you can put on when it's cold and then take off and put in your pocket or pack when things start to warm up. They make them for warming purposes and also make thinner ones for sun protection.

- **Socks** – There are also mountain biking specific socks you can get that will provide your feet with more comfort while keeping them cooler or warmer at the same time. These socks will come in a variety of sizes\lengths as well as thicknesses and materials. You can wear short socks to keep yourself cool or longer socks that go up your leg to offer protection from the cold and also from rubbing up against bushes.

  These socks are made from synthetic materials such as nylon and polyester and are woven much tighter together, allowing the socks to better conform to the shape of the foot and wick away moisture more effectively. Some will even have antibacterial fibers woven into the sock to kill germs and keep them from smelling too bad!

Shoes

Since your legs are providing the power via your feet to keep yourself moving on your bike, it's important to have the right kind of shoes to get the job done effectively and efficiently. Going back to my story on just wearing whatever I had on that day for my rides, the same goes for my shoes. I liked to use low cut hiking boots when riding because they provided a better grip on my pedals and allowed me to walk up hills in situations where I couldn't ride up them.

The type of shoes you will use when riding will depend on what type of pedals you use. Generally, there are two categories: flat pedals and clipless pedals. Flat pedals (or platform pedals, as they are commonly called) are the type where you place your foot on the pedal itself at whatever position feels comfortable to you. Clipless pedals are when you connect the bottom of your shoe to your pedal so it's attached as you ride. I will go into more detail about pedals in Chapter 6, and also explain why you clip into clipless pedals!

As you can see in the image below, we have some flat pedals with their associated shoes as well as some clipless pedals with their shoes.

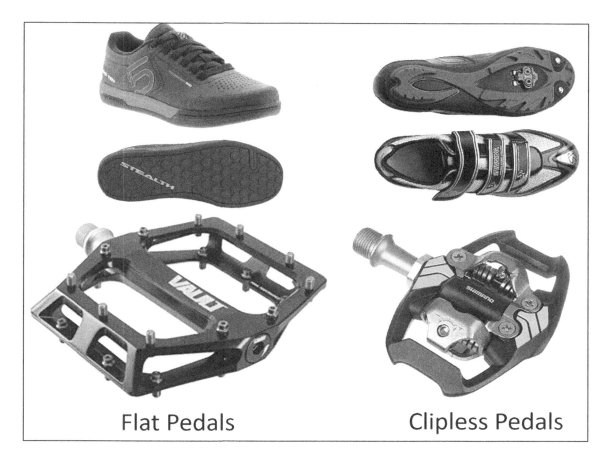

Flat Pedals   Clipless Pedals

If you are new to mountain biking, I would start with flat pedals because you don't want to have to worry about getting your feet off your pedals in case you need to put them on the ground really quickly in an emergency.

When it comes to flat pedal shoes there are many to choose from, and the prices go from reasonably priced to pretty expensive. They can also be made out of different materials, such as canvas or leather. Each type will wear differently, and some are more waterproof than others. You want to find a pair that are comfortable and fit snugly yet are not cutting off your circulation. Also, be sure that they are comfortable to walk in since you will most likely be using them to push your bike up a hill from time to time. The sole of the shoe is what's most important, and it needs to grip onto the pegs on the pedals so your feet don't slip off the pedals while riding. I have always been a fan of Five Ten brand shoes because they have one of the stickiest soles in the business, and their shoes are very comfortable.

Many of the same attributes apply to clipless shoes, but what's most important is how they feel when clipped into your pedals. You also need to make sure you have the same types of clips installed on your shoes that match the type of pedal you are using. The clips will screw onto the bottom of the show, allowing you to run various types and also replace them if necessary.

Gloves

Most people wear gloves when riding their mountain bikes, even though you will occasionally see people out on the trail with no gloves. Gloves help to keep your grip on your grips and also provide padding to prevent blisters and cushion your hands when things get rough.

There are ride-specific gloves (such as cross country gloves and downhill gloves), and each one is suited to that riding style. For example, with downhill gloves, they will always be full fingered and have more padding on the palm and also on the knuckles to protect them in case of a crash or run in with a branch or tree. Cross country gloves might be fingerless, not have as much padding, and may be made of a lighter weight material.

I like to have multiple sets of gloves for various conditions. I use fingerless gloves for most of my rides because they are comfortable and cooler since I live in a warm climate. I do have some full finger gloves for winter riding and some downhill gloves for things like bike parks when the risk of a high speed crash is greater. I have found that you don't need to spend a lot of money or buy name brand stuff to get some decent gloves, so shop around and experiment with some cheaper gloves and see how you like them.

Helmet

When it comes to shopping for accessories, your helmet is one of those items that you don't want to skimp on since it can be the difference between walking away from a crash and going to the hospital.

There are different types of bike helmets, so it won't be a one size fits all type of purchase. The types of helmets are basically broken up into three different categories.

Cross Country   All Mountain   Full Face

- **Cross Country** – These will be a lighter weight, more comfortable helmet with a more streamlined design with good ventilation. They offer good protection, but not as much as the other types of helmets.

- **All Mountain** – These are designed for more aggressive riding where you will be taking on more challenging trails with an increased risk of crashing. The main difference between all mountain and full face helmets is that the all mountain helmets will go down further on the back of your head, offering you more protection in that area. They also have a little more side protection as well.

- **Downhill\Full Face** – If you plan on doing some really crazy riding or visiting a place like a bike park, then you will need a full face helmet. These offer the most protection because they cover your entire head like a motorcycle helmet and will also protect you in front fall if you land on your face. They are not as comfortable as the other types but really aren't too bad because you generally aren't doing much pedaling at places like bike parks where they take you up the hill on a lift.

Sizing is important when choosing a helmet, so it's best to try them on locally rather than buy one online. Cross country and all mountain helmets will have an adjustable headband type component where you can make them tighter or looser around your head, and then also there will be strap adjustments that go around your chin. Some of the cheaper helmets are a one size fits all, but I would spend the money on a good one and get it in your actual size. You can usually find sizing charts for helmets that use the measurement around your head to match the size, especially for full face helmets that don't have the same adjustments.

The latest and greatest in helmet safety is called MIPS. MIPS stands for Multi-Directional Impact Protection System and is designed to provide protection against the rotational motion caused by angled impacts to the head which can result in brain injury. Rotational impacts are more dangerous to the head than linear impacts. MIPS technology was developed in Sweden in 1996 and is becoming a major factor in helmet design. This improved level of protection is accomplished by adding a layer between the EPS foam and your head. This layer moves about 10 to 15 mm in any direction to reduce the rotational motion from angled impacts and will allow the head to continue in the direction to which it was originally heading without transferring the rotational energies to the brain. MIPS works by mimicking the brain's own protection system with this type of movement, so look for a helmet that is MIPS certified for the best level of protection.

Pads
As you get better at riding and start to try out some more dangerous trails, sometimes it's good to have a little extra protection in case of a crash. In fact, you might want to even consider wearing some pads while you are getting used to riding your bike. There is nothing worse than taking a long trip to ride somewhere new and then crashing right at the start and hurting yourself and having to sit out while your friends are out there having fun.

There are different levels of pads for different types of riding, so don't go thinking you need to dress up like a hockey goalie just to have some protection on your local trails. The main difference is the material they are made of. For the more aggressive type of pads, you will find that they use hard plastic to protect areas such as your elbows, knees, and shins. They will feel bulkier and you will notice them while you are riding, but for the most part they are used for downhill runs where you get a ride to the top and just ride down. If you are getting really crazy, you can also get things like flak jacket type armor and also pads for your shoulders.

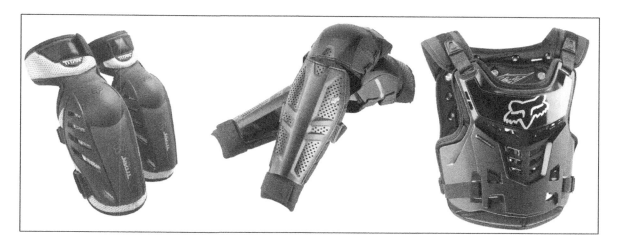

For the basic protection that you can wear all day long, the pads will be lighter and the protection zones will be made of foam or some kind of gel so they are more forgiving when you move. They can slip on for a snug fit, or some might even have straps to secure them.

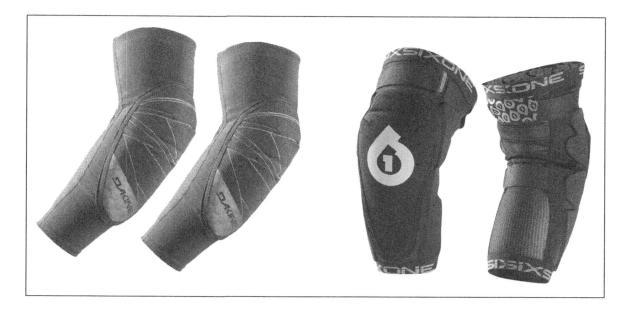

It might be a good idea to get yourself some basic lightweight pads if you are just starting out, so you don't get discouraged if you hurt yourself on a fall.

Glasses

Eye protection is very important when mountain biking because there will be a lot of dirt and other debris flying around when you are riding, especially if you are behind someone. If you want to wear your regular sunglasses that is fine, but there are better options for mountain biking eye protection.

You can get biking glasses that are lightweight and wrap around your face to give you more coverage when riding. Plus you don't need to worry about ruining your expensive sunglasses but instead can worry about ruining your expensive riding glasses. (Actually, you can get a decent pair of riding glasses for $40.)

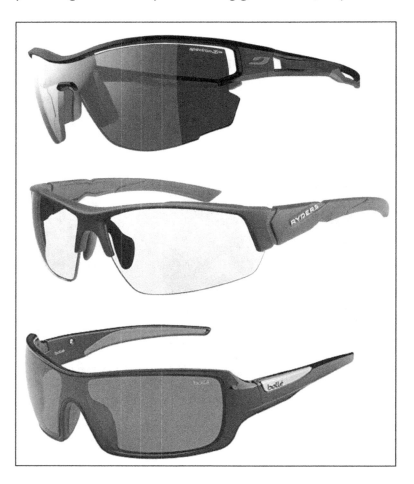

Many of these glasses will come with removable lenses so you can replace them if they get scratched or change them from a dark tint to a colored tint or even clear. I like to use glasses that have what they call photochromic lenses, which will be clear in the dark and then automatically get darker in the sunshine. That way I can use the same pair for bright light riding, night riding, and also riding in the trees where you have light and dark areas.

Whatever you do, get a pair that is light and comfortable, because it's not fun having heavy glasses weighing down on your nose during a long ride. You might have to spend a bit more money to get something nice and light, but it's worth it in the long run.

Water bottles
Hydration is super important when it comes to riding. Once you run out of water, then everything goes downhill fast, especially on hot days. If you don't carry a hydration pack (discussed next), then you will need to carry a water bottle in a water cage on your frame. There are many brands of water bottles to choose from and in a variety of sizes, so make sure you get one that fits within your frame because not every bottle will fit in every frame. In fact, shock position can greatly affect what size bottle you can use and if you can even fit one in your frame at all.

There will be threaded holes in the frame where the bottle cage will be attached, so that is the location you are stuck with unless you find another method such as a way to strap the bottle to your frame, or use a handlebar or seat mounted bottle holder.

I would avoid using generic bottled water bottles to hold your water since they are flimsy and for the most part are not the right size for a bottle cage. Plus, they won't stay cold for too long because there is no insulation. I like to use the CamelBak Podium Chill bottles since they are insulated and keep your water colder longer. You can even add some ice cubes when you fill it up to keep it colder even longer. They come in a couple of different sizes and a large variety of colors, so, if you like, you can even color coordinate it with your bike.

Of course, there are other brands that make similar bottles, so you can shop around to find exactly what you need.

Backpacks

Backpacks come in handy to carry things like water, food, tools, inner tube, keys, your phone, and maybe even a lightweight jacket. The downside of wearing a backpack is having to carry the extra weight on your back, and it makes you more uncomfortable on hot days because it will make your back sweat more than if you weren't wearing one.

I usually just stick with my water bottle in my cage and maybe a snack in my pocket for short rides to avoid the hassle. I have had to walk a few times because I got a flat or had some other issue and didn't have my tools or a spare tube with me, but that's the chance I take for comfort.

There are many bike-specific backpacks that are lightweight and designed to strap to your back with minimal discomfort. If you keep its contents to just what you need, then you will be more comfortable on long rides. You can always adjust what you are bringing based on the ride you are doing. You can get one with minimal storage space or one with all sorts of pockets to carry everything you could possibly need.

These backpacks will also have an internal water bladder that you can use to carry your water in addition to a bottle or instead of a bottle. There will be a hose that goes over your shoulder that you use to suck the water out of the bladder. You can also put ice in the bladder as well to keep it cooler. Below, you will see a sample of the many types and sizes of backpacks you can get, plus what the internal water bladder looks like.

The bladders are replaceable because eventually they will get old and run down and it's nice to have a new one once in a while. It's also important to clean them periodically and always drain them and let them dry out after each use. You can buy a special hanger that will open the bladder up and allow it to dry out on the inside. For cleaning, there are special solutions you can use, but I like to run hot soapy water through mine (including the tube) and then rinse it out with more hot water and let it dry.

Pump\Tools

There are several tools you can buy to keep your bike maintained even if you don't plan on doing all of the maintenance on your bike yourself. In fact, there are so many bike tools available that most people probably can't afford to own all of them! However, I feel there are a few must haves that every bike owner should have in their toolbox.

- **Tire Pump** – If you plan on riding more than once, then you will need a tire pump because tires don't stay fully inflated forever, even if you don't have a leak. Over time they will slowly lose air pressure, and it's always a good idea to check your tire pressure before every ride or maybe every couple of rides, assuming it hasn't been a long time in between them. You can get a tire pump with or without a built in gauge, so you know how much pressure is in your tire. Many of these gauges are not super accurate, but they will give you an idea of where you are at. You might also want to get a portable tire pump to take in your backpack or strap onto your bike frame for filling your tires on the trail.

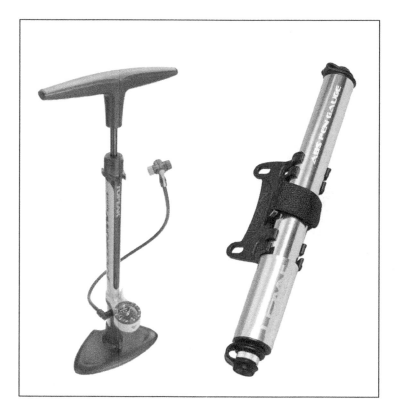

- **Air Pressure Gauge** – I like to use a dedicated digital air pressure gauge to check my tire pressure after using my floor pump because I like to have specific pressure in my tires and don't trust the gauge on my floor pump. These gauges are not too expensive and can even be used on your car tires if needed.

- **Shock Pump** – Your fork and shock air pressure needs to be checked periodically as well, and it requires a special pump that can pump up the high pressure that forks and shocks require without adding too much air too quickly. There are many brands to choose from, and some have analog gauges, and some have digital gauges and will cost a little bit more money.

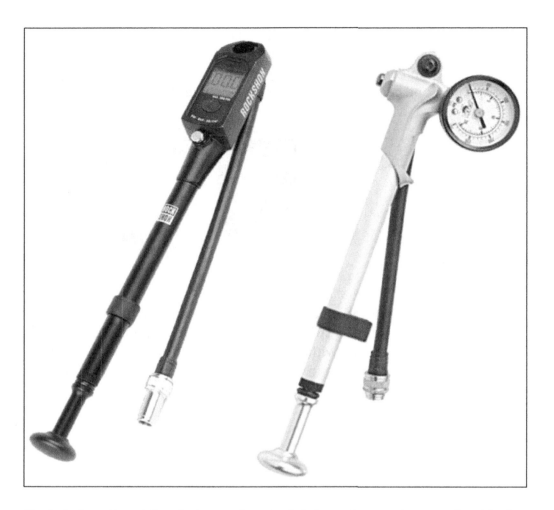

- **Chain Lube** – Your bike chain needs to be lubricated to work properly with the rest of your drivetrain. If it's not lubricated, then it will stiffen up and you will get noise coming from the chain and your bike will not shift as well as it should. There are many upon many types and brands of chain lube from wet to dry and wax to ceramic, so the conditions you ride in will determine what type of chain lube you should use.

- **Chain Cleaner** – Keeping your chain lubricated is great, but after a while, it will start to collect a lot of dirt, which gets in all the small crevices of the chain and is hard to get out with just a rag. This is where a good chain cleaner tool will help you out. These tools hold a cleaning solvent and brushes, and you run the chain through them to get it nice and clean. You don't need to do this each time you clean your chain, but maybe after every twenty rides or so.

- **Bike Cleaner** – Not only should you keep your chain clean, but you need to clean the other components of the drivetrain and even the frame and wheels, etc. once in a while. You can buy drivetrain specific cleaner that you can use on things like your chain, cassette, derailleur, and chainring. You can also buy cleaner that is designed to clean things like your frame, wheels, and so on to make your bike look like new again. If you ride in a lot of mud you might want to invest in a brush cleaning kit so you don't have to hose off your bike (which is not good for it in the long run).

- **Work Stand** – If you plan to do any kind of maintenance to your bike, you should consider investing in a work stand. This way you can get your bike off the ground, making it easier to work on and allowing you to do things like spin the wheels freely or even remove the wheels if needed. Using a bike stand even makes things like lubricating your chain much easier. Many will even come with a built in tool holder so you don't have to worry about finding the right tool for the job.

- **Tire Levers** – Flat tires are just a way of life when it comes to mountain biking, and when they happen they need to be fixed, otherwise the ride will be over. Tire levers are used to assist you in taking the tire off and putting the tire back on after fixing a flat or replacing an inner tube. There are all sorts of different styles made from things like plastic or metal, and it's kind of a trial and error process to see which kind works best for you. Good thing they are not super expensive!

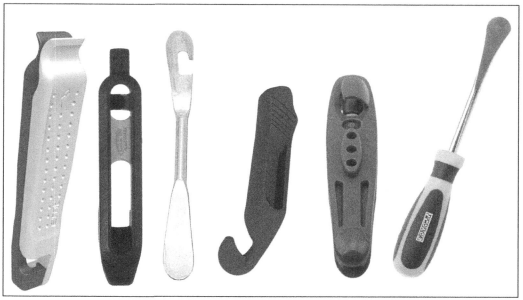

- **Chain Tool** – Chain tools are used to remove the pins from the chain when you need to separate the links to repair the chain while out on the trail. Most chains these days have what is called a master link, which is a link that can be removed by hand or with a link removal tool in order to remove the chain from the bike without damaging it or to shorten a new chain before putting it on your bike. It also allows you to reinstall the chain easily.

Chain removal tools will ruin the link that you use them on, so they are mainly used for chain repair on the trail. Once you push a pin out, then it is out for good.

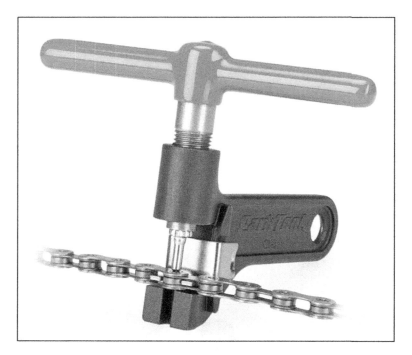

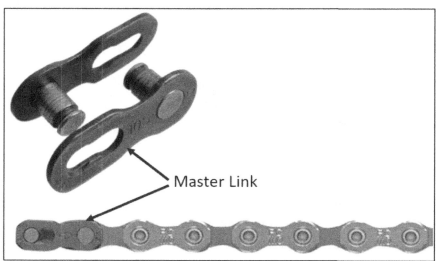

Master Link

It's always a good idea to have a spare master link with you in case you break your chain because you will need one to fix it. Then you will have two master links on your chain unless it's the master link itself that broke. Once you break a chain, it's a good idea to replace it rather than ride around with a "patched" one. Just be sure to get the right one for your chain. So, if you have a ten speed rear cassette, you will need a ten speed master link, and so on. Count the rings in your cassette if you are unsure how many speeds it is.

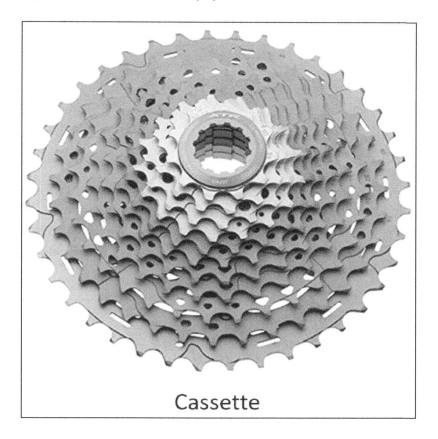

Cassette

- **Allen\Hex Wrenches** – Most bikes use Allen head or hex head bolts for most of their components, and for the most part they are metric sized bolts, so it's a good idea to have a set of Allen\hex wrenches in case you need to repair something or even tighten a loose bolt.

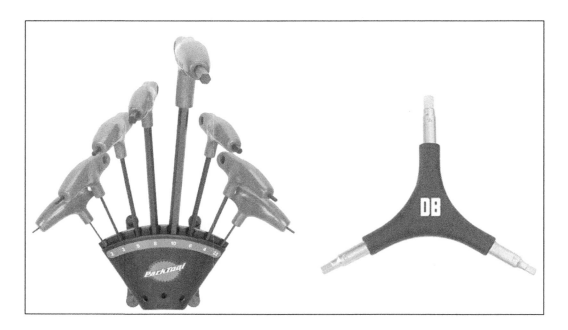

There are three main size bolts that are used on mountain biking for a lot of the components, and they are the 3, 4, and 5mm sizes. You can get an all-in-one tool like the one shown above that will contain all three sizes that you can take in your pack to handle most of the bolts on your bike. This doesn't mean that it will work for all of them, though, so keep that in mind.

GPS

Once you get some more experience on your mountain bike, you will want to go out and explore new areas or venture off farther on your local trails than you would normally go. If that's the case, and you are not a fan of getting lost, then you might want to try using a GPS (Global Positioning Satellite) on your rides.

Using a GPS will allow you to see exactly where you are while you are riding, and can also give you information about many other things, such as:

- Elevation gain
- Current elevation
- Available routes
- Turn by turn navigation
- Strava integration (discussed in Chapter 8)
- Rider to rider messaging

- The ability to see text messages and missed calls from your phone
- Training programs
- Performance monitoring

There are various makes and models to choose from with monochrome or color screens, as well as bike mounting accessories. Garmin is one of the top brands when it comes to cycling GPS units, but there are others to choose from as well.

Once you start tracking your rides and performance, you will find it addicting to see how you are progressing and also to see how you compare to your friends. It's the best way to get mountain biking bragging rights!

Lights
One cool thing about mountain biking is that you can do it 24 hours a day thanks to the modern lighting that you can mount on your bike or on your helmet so you can actually see where you are going on the trail at night.

These lights are more than just flashlights with a handlebar mount and are actually very bright and effective if you get the right one. You can either get one that has an external battery that you either strap to your frame or strap to your arm and then it will have a cable that attaches to the light.

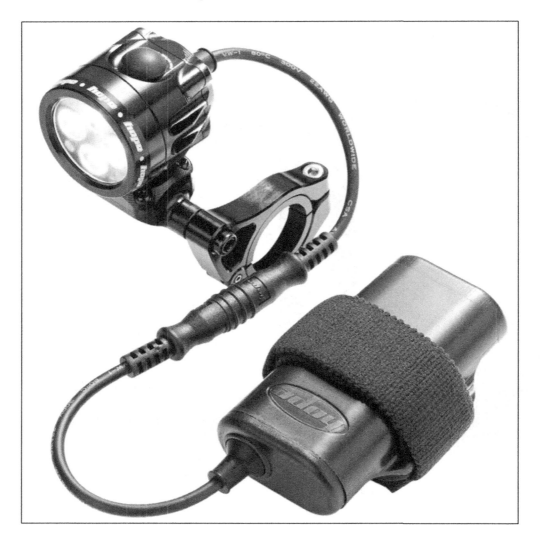

Or you can go for the type that is self-contained, which will look more like a flashlight because the battery is in the actual light itself.

The lights with external batteries tend to be more powerful, but the lights with internal batteries are easier to manage.

For the most part, you will mount the light on your handlebars, but some people like to mount the light on top of their helmet so when they turn their head the light will follow where they are looking.

Then you have people who like to have a light on the handlebars as well as one on their helmet. I have used the dual light method before and like it, while others have said they don't like the way it works.

When it comes to choosing a light, it mostly comes down to lumens, which is the number that basically tells you how bright the light is. I would try and get a light that is over 1,000 lumens if it's your main light. If you want to add an additional light on your helmet, then you can save yourself some money and go for a lower power light such as one that is maybe 500 lumens.

The bulbs and lenses will also make a difference in how the light works. I find that the lights with dual lenses give off a wider beam compared to the single lens lights, which tend to be more focused.

Be sure to do your homework and read reviews on a bunch of lights before making your decision. Even an expensive light can turn out to have average performance, so it's always a good idea to let other people test them out for you!

Chapter 6 – Bike Components

Frame

The frame is the heart of your bike, and the style you choose along with its geometry will determine how the bike will ride and what types of trails it will handle the best. As I discussed in Chapter 3, there are various types of mountain bikes, and the frame will determine what category it falls under.

If you want to build your own bike, you can just buy the frame and then customize it with whatever components you desire. Keep in mind that some bike manufacturers will not sell their frames by themselves, so if that's the case, you would have to look for a used one (which might be the better option anyway). When you buy the frame, it will usually come with the shock included, but that can always be swapped out if you like. You will need to choose a shock that is the same size as the one you are replacing so it will fit. Some bike manufacturers will use proprietary shocks, meaning that most aftermarket shocks won't fit.

Frames have different geometry, which refers to things like the length and angles of certain things like the top tube, seat tube, wheelbase length, etc. As you can see in the image below, things can get complicated, and these aren't even all the measurements you can apply to a bike's geometry.

Don't get intimidated by all of these measurements, because for the most part, you won't need to worry about them as long as the bike feels right to you.

As for frame materials, I had mentioned that you can get an aluminum frame, carbon fiber frame, or a mixture of both. It all depends on how much you want to spend and how light you want to go. On average, a carbon frame will save you around 1 to 1.5 lbs. in weight, which is a lot in terms of mountain biking weight. For a cross country or trail bike, you want to see if you can keep the total weight under 30 lbs. or so.

Drivetrain

The drivetrain on a mountain bike is what gets the bike in motion and keeps it moving. It consists of several parts that need to work together to transfer your leg power into wheel power. The image below shows the main components of a mountain bike drivetrain.

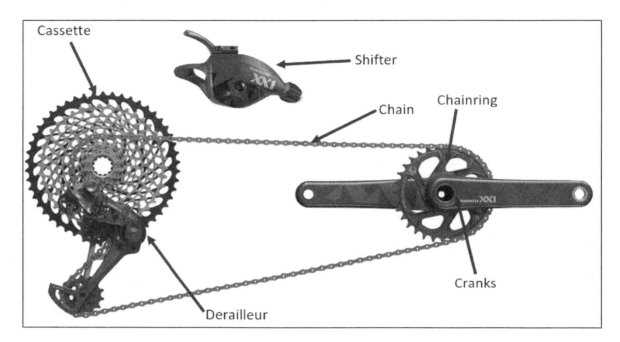

Each component has a specific job, and if any one of them fails, then there is a good chance your day of riding is ruined. Plus, the nicer the drivetrain, the smoother it shifts and pedals and the less it weighs. You can get things like the cranks and derailleur in carbon fiber as well.

- **Cranks** – Think of the cranks as being similar to the crankshaft in your engine, assuming you know what that is! The cranks connect to the frame and have arms that you bolt your pedals into so you can transfer the power of your legs through the chain to the rear wheels. The crank arms come in different lengths if you need something shorter or longer. As you can see in the image above, there are two holes in the crank arms, and that is where the pedals go.

- **Chain** – The chain is pretty self-explanatory and is used to transfer the power from the cranks to the cassette in the rear. There are specific size chains based on how many speeds your bike is, so when it comes time to replace it, make sure you get the right type.

- **Chainring** – The chainring bolts on to the cranks and is what the chain grabs on to in order to move the cassette in the rear and, therefore, the rear wheel. You can get them in different sizes to make pedaling easier going uphill or to allow you to go faster. The sizes go by the number of teeth, so a 32 tooth (32T) chainring is smaller than a 38 tooth (38T) chainring. The 32T chainring will be easier to climb with, but the 38T will allow you to go faster without maxing out your legs by having them spin faster than you can pedal. Back in the old days, mountain bikes would have three chainrings in the front, and then it went down to two. Now it's most common to only have one chainring in the front. You can also get an oval shaped chainring, which is supposed to help smooth out your power delivery on hill climbs. (You can only use an oval chainring when you have just one chainring on your bike.)

- **Cassette** – The cassette is made up of many different size chainrings connected together, allowing you to change how easy or hard it is to pedal based on which one you are using. It works the opposite as the front chainring because the bigger the ring you are in, the easier it is to pedal uphill, and the smaller ones are used for speed on downhills. To calculate the number of speeds your bike has, simply multiply the number of rings in your cassette by the number of chainrings up front. So, if you have two chainrings up front and ten chainrings in your cassette, then your bike has twenty speeds. Most bikes now are going with one ring up front and twelve rings in the cassette. They are referred to as one by twelve drivetrains.

- **Shifter** – This is the lever that mounts on the handlebars that allow you to change gears up and down based on whether you need to use an easier gear for a climb or a faster gear for more speed.

- **Derailleur** – The derailleur is responsible for shifting gears when you change gears using the shifter. It will use a cable connected to the shifter mounted on the handlebars, and then move the chain to a bigger or smaller ring depending on which way you move the shifter lever. There are also wireless derailleurs that don't use a cable but they require you to have a battery in the shifter as well as the derailleur and are a more expensive option.

Suspension
If it wasn't for suspension on mountain bikes, they would pretty much be road bikes with big, knobby tires on them. And when I say *suspension*, I am referring to the fork in the

front and the shock in the rear. As I mentioned before, there are bikes called hardtails that don't have a shock in the rear, and the ones that do are called full suspension bikes.

The suspension is responsible for absorbing bumps just like the shock absorbers do on your car and actually work in a similar fashion. Not all shocks and forks are the same, and there are different levels of performance and features available with these suspension components.

Fork
The fork is responsible for smoothing out the ride at the front of the bike. It also connects the front wheel to the frame, and you also connect the handlebars to the fork so you can turn the front wheel.

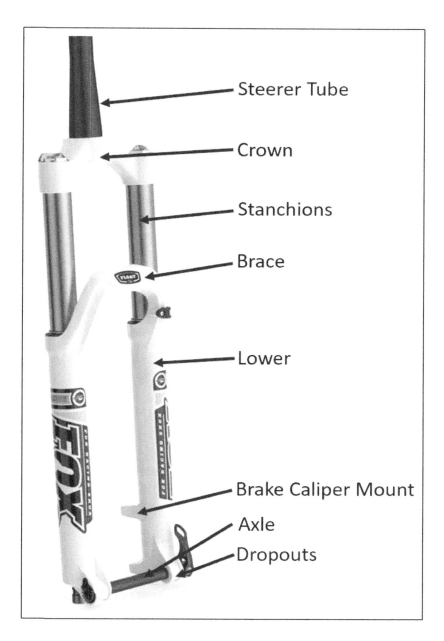

I will now go over the parts that make up a suspension fork.

- **Steerer Tube** – The steerer tube is what connects the handlebars and stem to the fork and allows you to steer the bike. They come in different lengths, so sometimes they have to be cut down if they are too long, otherwise you will have too much tube sticking out of the top tube part of your frame.

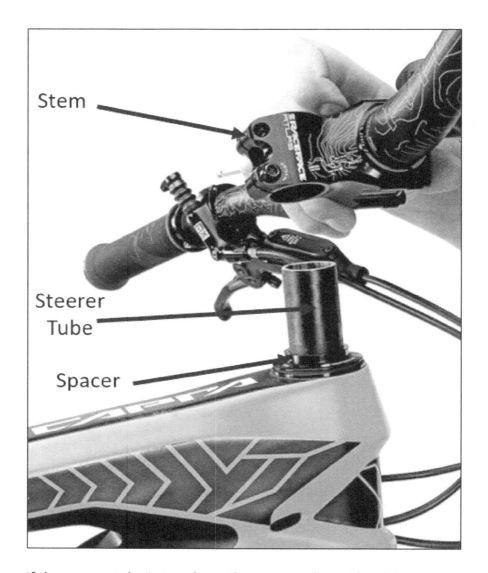

If the steerer tube is too short, then you might not be able to mount your stem to it or be able to use the right number of spacers to get the stem and handlebars to the height you need them to be. Of course, when you buy a bike as a whole, the steerer tube will be cut down to the proper length already. There can be an exception where it's still too short for your settings compared to the previous owner or factory settings. Having to cut down your steerer tube will usually only apply to buying a new fork for your bike. Then again, it might be the right size right out of the box. Also keep in mind that there are different types of steerer tubes such as tapered and oversized. For most bikes, the size is 1 $^{1/8}$ inches, with older bikes having a 1 inch tube.

- **Crown** – The crown is the arched piece that connects the steerer tube to the rest of the fork via the stanchions. The top of the crown will also be where some of your fork adjustment knobs are located, such as for compression and lockout (discussed later). You will also find the Schrader air valve located on the crown, which is where you connect your shock pump to add or remove air from your fork.

- **Stanchions** – Stanchions will travel in and out of the lower body of the fork, giving you the travel and movement you need to cushion your ride. They contain internal components such as a spring or air chamber, damper rod, oil, and valves. It's a good idea to clean your stanchions between rides to avoid extra dirt getting in the internal workings of the fork, which will affect the way it performs and require you to have it serviced sooner. Stanchions come in various sizes\thicknesses such as 32mm, 34mm, 36mm, and so on. The forks that are designed for more aggressive bikes will have thicker stanchions so they can take more abuse. However, these forks will weigh more.

- **Brace** – The brace is what helps to secure both sides of the fork and keep everything together and rigid. The crown also helps with this task.

- **Lower** – The lower is what the stanchions slide into, and will move up and down as you ride over bumps. It is also the part that your wheel will connect to. They contain wiper seals that keep dirt, dust, and contaminants out of the internals of your fork.

- **Brake Caliper Mount** – In order to have front brakes on your bike, they need to be mounted somewhere secure, and this is why they are connected to the lower section of the fork. Forks will have a built in brake caliper mount to allow the brakes to be securely mounted to the bike.

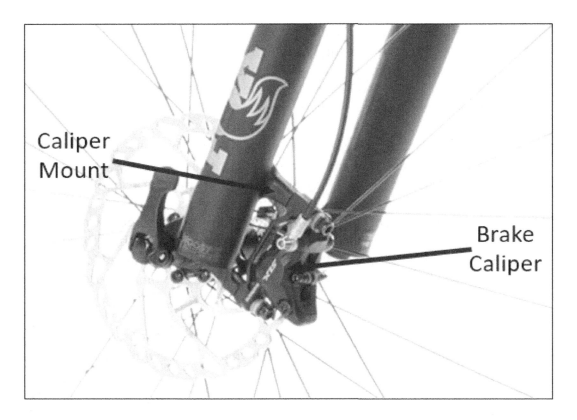

- **Axle** – The axle (often called through axle) is what goes through the hub of the wheel and the dropouts on the fork and screws into one of the dropouts. There are different sizes of axles, and they need to match up with the hub of the wheel and the distance between the dropouts.

- **Dropouts** – These are the mounting points for the wheel on the fork and where the axle will screw into in order to secure the wheel.

Depending on what shock or fork you end up with, you will have certain levels of adjustment that you can use to fine tune how your suspension works. The main adjustments you will make to your fork are as follows:

- **Air Pressure** – All forks will come with a recommended air pressure based on the model of the fork and your weight. It's to be used as a starting point, and then you can increase the pressure or decrease the pressure to fine tune how it feels to you. Don't go too far in either direction to avoid damaging your internal components. The air spring is the internal component that resists the weight of the rider. Higher air pressure can be used to provide firmer compression and minimize bottoming out of the fork. Lower air pressure can be used to provide a more supple feel over bumps.

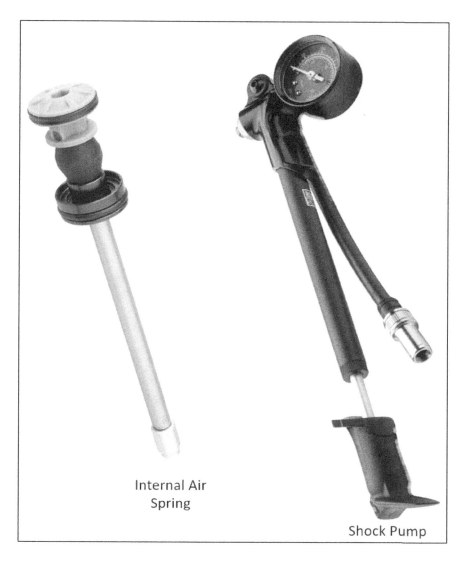

Internal Air
Spring

Shock Pump

The same air pressure won't feel this same on totally different types of terrain, so you may find yourself needing to adjust it depending on where you are riding.

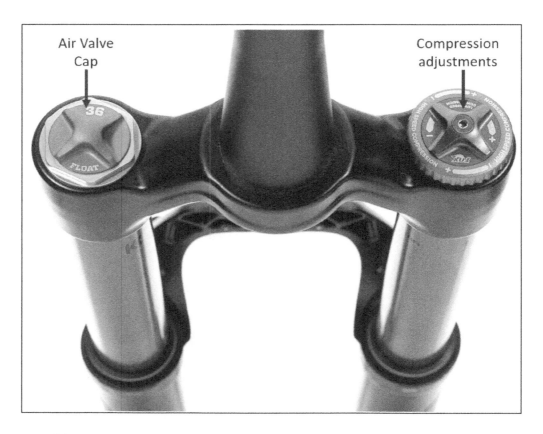

To add air to your fork you will need to find the air valve (which is usually the Schrader type), attach your shock pump, and add air to get to the required pressure (PSI). It is usually located under a removable cap that you can unscrew on the top of the fork crown.

- **Compression** – Not all forks will have compression settings, and they are usually reserved for higher end forks and forks that go on Enduro and Downhill bikes since they can befit the most from changing compression settings.

Compression settings pretty much do what they are named after—they control how much your suspension compresses under what type of load. If you don't have enough compression damping, your bike will bob around and blow through its travel on descents and under hard braking. When you have too much compression damping this will prevent your suspension from absorbing impacts effectively, and you will notice your bike springing back, trying to buck you off of it.

Some forks will have knobs where you can fine tune the compression by turning the knob one way or the other. Other forks will have preset compression settings where you can choose a mode that works best for the situation. For example, many forks will have a climb, trail, and descend setting, where climb is the stiffest and descend is the softest and you can just flip the lever based on what you are riding. These are often called Pro Pedal settings. Higher end forks will have both a low-speed and high speed compression adjustment.

- **Rebound** – Rebound damping is what controls the speed at which your suspension re-extends or recovers after absorbing a bump. Setting your rebound can be difficult and requires a lot of trial and error to get things just right. Then, once you get it right, it doesn't mean it will perform its best on every trail, and you might need to change the settings to match the trail.

The rebound knob is usually found at the bottom of the right fork leg and will be red in color. It should have a sticker with a + or − sign indicating faster or slower, or it might have a picture of a rabbit for faster and a turtle for slower.

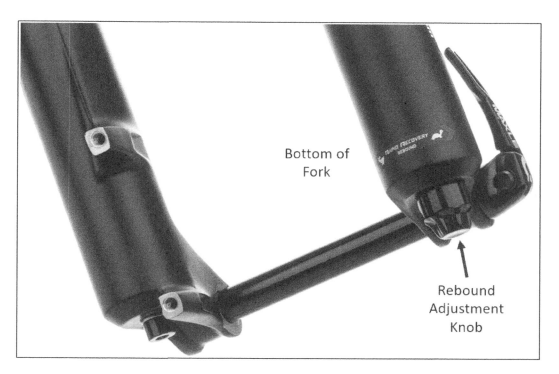

Not enough rebound will make your suspension act like a pogo stick and bounce you around all over the place on rougher terrain. Too much rebound will cause your suspension to pack down and not be responsive enough, which will result in a harsher ride. If you go online and read about how to adjust your rebound settings, you will hear opinions that are all over the place. What I like to do is pick a nice downhill section of a trail that has the type of terrain I usually ride on and then ride down it over and over with different settings until I find the setting I like. Just keep track of how many clicks you are out from the fastest setting and then adjust from there. Only move two or three clicks at a time and then re-test. Higher end forks will have both a low speed and high speed rebound adjustment.

Shock

The shock serves the same purpose as the fork does—minus the attaching of the wheel for turning purposes. Its job is to absorb the shocks from bumps at the rear of the bike. It works in a similar fashion, but where it is placed in the frame is different depending on what brand of bike it's being used on. Some manufacturers like to use a vertical type design while others prefer a more horizontal positioning.

There are pivot points placed at specific locations that allow the rear of the frame to move in unison with the shock and absorb the bumps and therefore smooth out the ride at the rear of the bike.

The components of a shock are similar to that of a fork, and you will find the same types of settings such as compression and rebound. You can get a shock that uses an air damper to do its thing, or one that uses a spring.

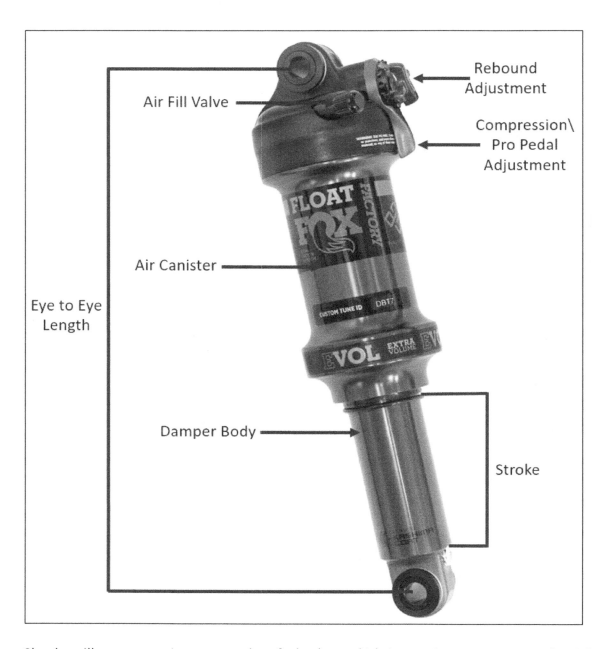

Shocks will use more air pressure than forks do, and it's just as important to get the right pressure in your shock just like your fork. A shock will most likely take over 200 psi to be properly pressurized whereas a fork might take around 70-90 psi.

You will also see some shocks with an extra canister, also known as a piggyback ore reservoir shock. The purpose of this extra canister is to help with performance by splitting the load of a shock between two compression circuits can make a shock feel less harsh and also keep things cooler when you are really giving your shock a workout.

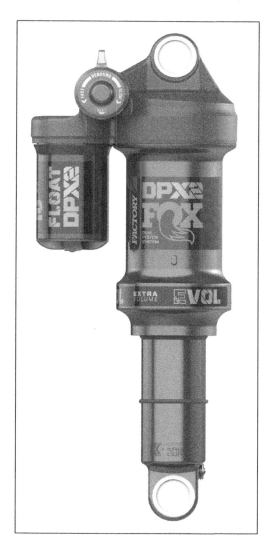

When replacing a shock, you will need to make sure that you get one that is the same size when it comes to the eye-to-eye length and damper body. Some bikes will only allow you to fit their own proprietary shock, which reduces your replacement options.

Pedals

In order to get the power from your legs to the cranks on the bike, you will need to use pedals to do so. Having the right type of pedal is important for ride comfort and performance. Plus, having a pedal that will keep your feet planted when things get rough is important as well.

You have two choices when it comes to pedal types, and they are flat pedals and clipless pedals. Each has its advantages, but if you ask anyone which is the way to go, they will always choose the type that they use!

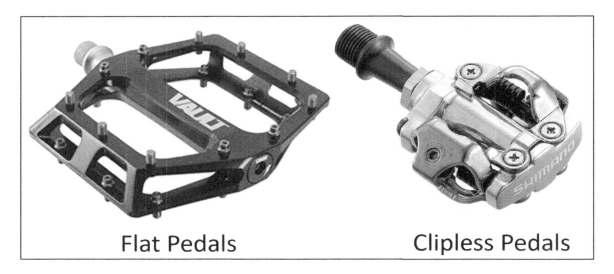

Flat Pedals   Clipless Pedals

Flat Pedals
Flat pedals (or platform pedals, as they are often called) are exactly that—platforms that you put your feet on to transfer power from your legs to the drivetrain. They have a spindle that threads into the crank arms to secure them to the cranks. They will have pins sticking out of them that are used to grip the bottom of your shoe to keep your feet planted. These pins are often screws that can be replaced if they break off on a rock or get too worn down and lose their grip.

The main benefit of flat pedals is that it is easy to get your feet off of them and on the ground when you need to do so in a hurry. Many downhill riders use flat pedals because of this, even though you are starting to see more and more downhill rides using clipless pedals. Flat pedals are also used for riders who do tricks where they need to remove their feet from the pedals for a particular trick.

You can get flat pedals in a variety of materials such as aluminum, magnesium, and plastic. The size and shape of flat pedals will vary from brand to brand as well. Higher end pedals can be rebuilt when they start to make noise or not spin freely, saving you money on replacing them. Be prepared to spend around $80 and up for some nice lightweight flat pedals. If you are new to mountain biking, I recommend you start with flat pedals to avoid unwanted injuries that can occur from being inexperienced with clipless pedals.

Clipless Pedals
Clipless pedals are used along with special shoes that clip into the pedal itself and secures your foot to the pedal. That way there is much less of a chance of your foot slipping off the pedal.

You might be wondering why pedals that you clip your shoes into are called clipless, and there is actually an explanation for how they got their name. Back in the early days of mountain biking, there were pedals where you slid your foot into the pedal and strapped it down. An example is shown below.

Then someone came up with the idea to get rid of the strap or foot cage in favor of having the bottom of the shoe connect to the pedal itself, and then decided to call these new pedals clipless. (Well, I guess it sort of makes sense where the name came from.)

Another benefit of using a clipless pedal besides keeping your feet on the pedal is that you get to apply power to the upstroke of the pedal stroke and not just the downstroke like you do with flat pedals. They also keep your feet in the appropriate position on the pedal at all times.

The downside to clipless pedals is that there is a chance you might end up falling down if you can't unclip your foot from the pedal fast enough. To unclip your foot, you need to rotate it on the pedal until it comes free. The clips on the pedal are adjustable as to how much tension it takes to disconnect. I have seen many times where someone is trying to make it up a really steep hill or over a technical section of the trail and can't unclip fast enough to put their foot down and end up falling on their side.

There are different styles and brands of clipless pedals, so make sure you get the cleats for the shoes that match the pedal type. Expect to pay around $60 or so for a decent set of clipless pedals.

Grips

When it comes to keeping your hands on the handlebars, grips will make a big difference in how that works out for you. It's important to choose the right set of grips for comfort and performance reasons.

Grips come in a variety of shapes, sizes, materials, and colors, so it might be a little overwhelming when trying to figure out what grips will work best for you. One thing you can do is go to a bike shop and feel what they have installed on their bikes to get an idea of what you might like. If you really want to experiment, you can wear your gloves to get an accurate feeling of what they will be like out on the trail.

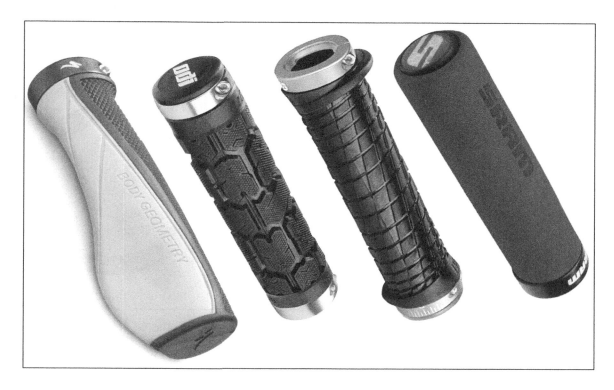

For the most part, grips will be made out of a rubber compound, but you will also find foam and even plastic grips. Thinner grips will give you a more direct feeling of the handlebars while thicker grips will offer more cushioning and shock absorption in your hands. I personally like to use the ODI Rogue grips because they are very "grippy" and have the right amount of thickness for my tastes.

Back in the old days, we used to lube up the insides of our grips with soapy water to help slide them on to the handlebars. Now grips will use a clamp-on style where you will have clamps on one or both ends of the grips to keep them in place so you can take them on and off easily.

Wheels

If there is one thing you need to get your bike moving, that would be the wheels. I talked about the different wheel sizes in Chapter 4 and will include the image showing the three main sizes in use today. Well, soon it will be down to two sizes since the 26 inch wheel isn't really used anymore except on older bikes or maybe a bike you would buy at Walmart!

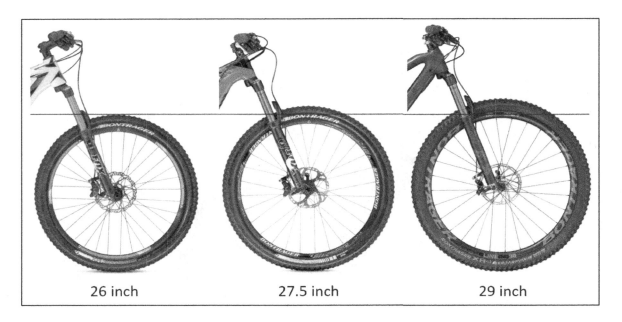

| 26 inch | 27.5 inch | 29 inch |

Wheels can be made of aluminum or carbon fiber, with carbon fiber being more expensive, yet lighter and stiffer than aluminum. One is not really better than the other since some people swear by aluminum wheels and others say carbon is the way to go.

There are three main parts to a mountain bike wheel that you should be aware of, and each part is just as important as the others. These parts of the wheel are the hoop, spokes, and the hub.

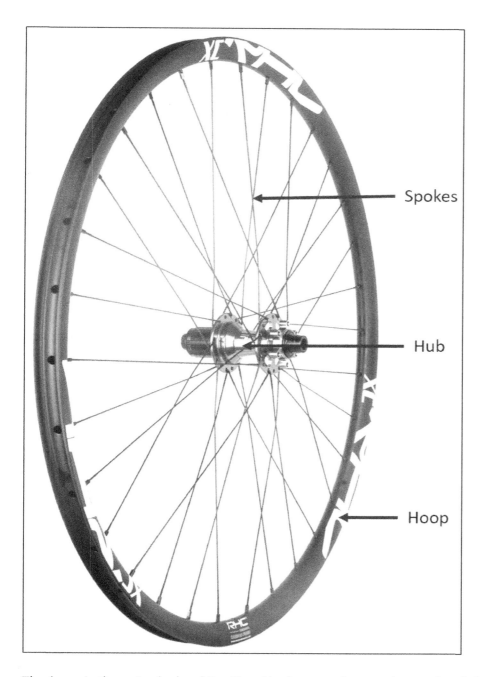

Spokes

Hub

Hoop

The *hoop* is the actual wheel itself and is the part that can be made of aluminum or carbon fiber. The hoops have holes in them that are used to connect the spokes that then connect to the hub. Most wheels use 32 spokes, but you can get some that use 24 spokes as well.

The *spokes* are what give the wheel its strength and connect the hoop to the hub. The spokes also transfer the power from the rider to make the wheel spin. Plus, they support your weight so you can sit on the bike without crushing the wheels themselves. There are different types of spokes that can be used on a bike wheel such as round or bladed. You use the type of spoke that is appropriate for the type of bike that they will be used with. If you use spokes made for a cross country bike on a downhill bike, then you will most likely be breaking some spokes. Fortunately, you can replace spokes if you break them, but they will have to be the same type and length as the ones you broke.

The *hub* is the part of the wheel that connects to the hoop via the spokes and allows the wheel to spin freely by using internal bearings. The axle will slide through the hub to hold it in place on the fork or on the frame and allow it to spin freely. Not all hubs are the same and are not something you want to go cheap on when replacing them or building yourself some custom wheels.

The rear hub contains what is called the *freewheel,* which is used to transfer power to the wheels by locking when pedaling forward and then spinning freely when you pedal backward. The cassette also connects to the rear hub.

Tires

Tires are one of those things where you will choose the type of tire you run based on the trail characteristics as well as your riding style. You might find that you will go through several makes and models of tires before finding the ones that work for you. It's good to start with the type that best suits the trails you will be riding on and then narrow it down to the model that works best for you.

Tires come in various widths with various tread patterns that can be made for mud, sand, rocks, loose dirt, hardpack, and so on. It's best to try and get a good compromise if you ride in various types of conditions. As you can see in the image below, you can get a really knobby tire for increased grip and ruggedness, or you can get one with a lighter tread pattern that can be used to move you along the trail faster and with less rolling resistance.

Tire width will also play a factor in tire performance. Generally the wider the tire, the better it is for technical terrain and things like Enduro and downhill riding. But on the downside, it's going to give you more resistance when pedaling and weigh more than a lighter, skinnier tire would.

The compound used in tires can vary as well and makes a difference in how rugged the tire is and how well it performs. If you plan on riding in rocky areas, then you want a tire with a more durable compound that is designed to take the abuse and not puncture as easily as a less durable tire. Mountain bike tires also contain woven in fibers to help contribute to their strength and can use extra material (called double ply) or even an armor type material to make them stronger.

Many people will run two different tires on their bikes so that they have one that offers a good grip up front and one that offers less rolling resistance out back. Sometimes they will even have a thinner tire in the back to keep them rolling faster and keep the weight down.

There are so many mountain bike tires available that it will make your head spin, and at $50 - $100 apiece, it's not something you want to have to buy over and over to find the one that works for you. So do your homework, research tires online, and check out what people have to say about them in reviews and on bike forums before opening up your wallet and spending your hard earned cash.

Brakes
Brake technology for bikes has come a long way since the old days of V-brakes (shown below) where rubber brakes pad would squeeze together against the outside of the wheel to make you stop. You will still find these types of brakes on very cheap mountain bikes like you would get in a store like Target. You will also find them on road bikes, but they are more advanced than they were years ago. Road bikes are now starting to come with disk brakes as well as newer technology that makes them lighter.

For the most part, you will be dealing with disk brakes on your mountain bike. There are two types, and they are mechanical and hydraulic. The main difference between the two is that mechanical disk brakes use a cable similar to your derailleur cable while hydraulic disc brakes use brake fluid like your car does.

Since mechanical brakes use a cable to apply the brakes (and just like with derailleur cables), they can get stretched out and dirty, which will affect braking performance. Mechanical brakes also don't stop as well as hydraulic brakes, but they can be easier to adjust since it's just a simple cable and doesn't cost as much to purchase. Some people even have issues with snapping cables on mechanical brakes, but I'm sure that's only in extreme cases.

Hydraulic brakes use brake fluid, and when you squeeze the brake lever it compresses the fluid and makes the brakes function. This method offers stronger and more reliable braking performance but will cost you more for the brakes themselves. You also have to worry about bleeding the brake fluid if their performance begins to suffer, and you also have to make sure to keep air out of the brake lines. Just like with car brakes, you will need to change the brake fluid every so often, but for the most part this will be pretty rare. Since hydraulic brakes are a sealed system, you don't have to worry about dirt and mud affecting your performance (unless you get your pads dirty, that is, but that goes the same for mechanical brakes as well).

You might hear the term *modulation* when talking about or reading about brakes. This refers to the amount of control or fine tuning you get when applying the brakes. Having more modulation means you can control the stopping power more precisely, but you usually need to pull the brake lever closer to the bars to get more stopping power when needed. Some people prefer less modulation and like the brakes to just come on strong when they pull the brake lever. SRAM brand brakes are known for their modulation while Shimano brakes are known to have much less modulation. Either way, it's simply a preference and it's up to you to decide what works best for your riding style.

There are four main components to the braking system on a bike with disk brakes. (Well, maybe six if you count the brake lines and fluid, but for now I won't!)

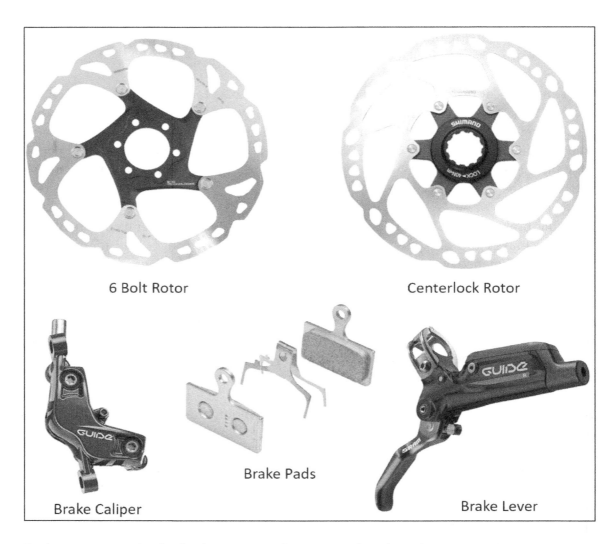

6 Bolt Rotor   Centerlock Rotor

Brake Pads

Brake Caliper   Brake Lever

Each component in the braking system has a specific job and is just as important as any of the other components, so that's why it's always a good idea to keep your braking system maintained.

- **Rotor** – Disk brake systems have rotors just like your car does, but on a smaller scale, of course. The rotor is attached to the hub of the wheel by either the more common six bolt design, or the Shimano Centerlock type. The rotor is what the brake pads clamp down on to apply braking pressure to slow you down or stop the bike.

Rotors come in different sizes and styles, so they are all not the same. The bigger the rotor (in diameter) the more stopping power you will have. Many bikes will have a slightly bigger rotor in the front than in the back. Higher end rotors are made of material designed to stay cool by dissipating heat so they can work more effectively since heat is the enemy of braking performance. Occasionally you will need to replace your rotors if they get too worn or get warped or bent. (It is possible to straighten a bent rotor if you have the patience to give it a try.)

- **Pads** – As I mentioned above, the brake pads are what clamp down onto the rotor on both sides to slow the bike down. As you use your brakes, the pads will wear down until they get to the point where you will need to replace them. For most normal riding conditions, this might be a once a year type of thing, but that will vary on how often you ride and how you use your brakes. Just be sure not to let the pads wear down to the rivets, otherwise you will end up damaging your rotor and having to replace that, too. When the thickness of the pads gets down to about the thickness of a dime, then it's time to replace them. A set of brake pads will run you around $20, and a router will cost around $60. Brake pads are one of those do-it-yourself types of jobs where after you do it the first time you realize how easy it is to do. The make and model of the brakes you have will determine how the process is done, but you can usually find instructions online or in a video on YouTube.

  Brake pads come in different materials and each type performs differently. The pads can be either metallic (sintered), or organic. Metallic pads have a metal compound in them and are good for wet and dirty conditions. They will generally last longer than organic pads. Organic pads are made from a high density ceramic. They are softer than metallic pads, and therefore have better stopping power and heat dissipation, but they will not last as long as metallic pads. They are also not as effective in wet conditions. I like to use organic pads because they are quieter than metallic, and there is nothing more annoying than squeaking brakes!

- **Caliper** – The caliper is the component that houses the brake pads and is responsible for squeezing them against the rotor to slow you down. When you squeeze the brake lever, it pushes the hydraulic fluid and causes the pistons in the caliper to push together on the pads. Not all calipers are the same, and you can get different levels of performance from different models. Some might have a two piston system while others have a four piston system (which provides better performance and would be used on a more aggressive performing bike). There is a caliper bolted to the fork for the front brakes, and then one bolted to the seat stay of the frame for the rear brakes.

- **Brake Levers** – Mountain bikes have front and rear brakes, and, therefore, front and rear brake levers. The left lever controls the front brake while the right lever controls the rear brake. This is the opposite of most motorcycles, so if you ride one, you might have to get used to things being backwards!

  The brake levers have reservoirs on them that contain brake fluid that is used to engage the brakes (unless you are using mechanical brakes, of course). On higher end brakes the lever is adjustable, so you can determine how far away it is from the handlebars to adjust the comfort level. You can also slide the brake levers up and down on the handlebars to adjust the positioning as well.

Keep in mind that how well your brakes work will also depend on the quality of the brakes, so if you buy a cheap set of hydraulic brakes, they most likely won't work as well as a good set of mechanical brakes. Another thing to keep in mind is rotor size and type of pads, since the larger the rotor the better the stopping power and less brake fade you will get. Brake fade is when the brakes get hot and don't work as well as they do when they are cooler. As I mentioned earlier, brake pad material varies too, with each type offering its own set of benefits.

Handlebars

You might think that handlebars are, well, just handlebars, but you would be wrong. Sure they all do the same thing, and that is let you steer your bike while giving you something to hold on to. But there are various types of handlebars that come in different shapes, sizes, and materials, so choosing the right type will affect how your bike performs.

Mountain bike handlebars come in different widths and thicknesses and have different angles to them, and all of these factors make a difference in how they feel on the trail. Back in Chapter 4, I mentioned handlebar width and rise, so now I will go into more detail about that along with the difference in thickness.

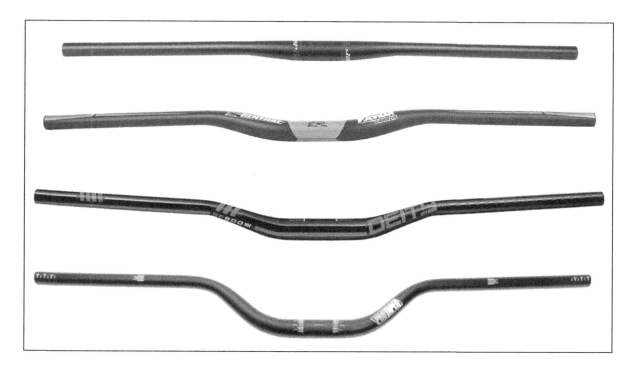

Choosing the right width will make a difference in how your bike handles out on the trail. Mountain bike handlebars have been getting wider over the years, but it seems as though they have finally maxed out and are not getting any bigger. Wider handlebars will be more stable at high speeds and offer more leverage when turning. Narrower bars are used more for cross country or XC race bikes where you are leaning over more and you want your arms tucked in for aerodynamic purposes. Your shoulder width will also make a difference in how a certain width handlebar will feel.

Handlebars are measured in millimeters, with 760mm being a good all-around width for mountain biking handlebars. Generally, downhill mountain bikers will go 780-800mm, and you will even see some bars as wide as 820mm. Personally, I like 780-800mm bars because they feel stable going fast downhill and also feel fine when climbing (at least to me).

Handlebar rise is another aspect of bar sizing that you should know about. The rise is how much the handlebars rise from flat measured in degrees. If you look at the image above of the four different handlebars, you will notice that the one on top is flat while the others have different degrees of rise to them. An average rise handlebar will have 10-30 degrees of rise to it. The amount of rise that you use will be determined by what feels best to you.

Bike manufacturers will try and put the correct type of bars on the bike from the factory based on what the bike is meant to be used for.

One other thing related to the rise of your handlebars is their backsweep and upsweep. Backsweep refers to the angle at which the bars swoop toward the back of the bike, while upsweep is the vertical angle of the bars at the grip.

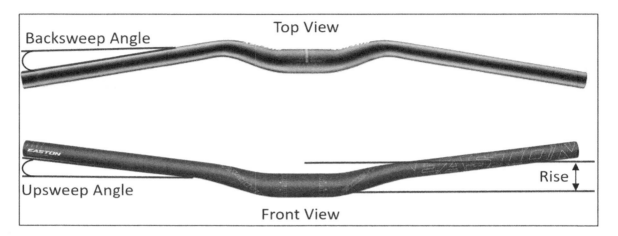

Finally, we have the handlebar thickness. This is the diameter of the handlebar where it connects to the stem. The most common diameter is 31.8mm, which you will find on most XC and trail bikes. But lately, the trend has been to increase the diameter to 35mm to provide greater strength and stiffness. You will see this a lot on Enduro and downhill bikes.

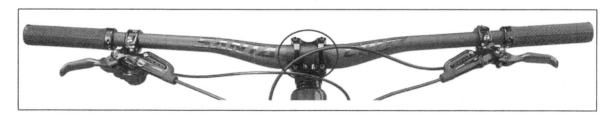

I use the 35mm bars myself and noticed a slight difference over the 31.8mm bars, so it might not be worth changing unless you happen to be changing your handlebars anyway for some other reason. Keep in mind that you will need to change your stem as well to match the larger size bars.

Seatpost
Mountain bike seatposts have come a long way since the days of them just being pretty much a hollow metal tube that you stuck in your frame and bolted your seat to. Now,

most people will use what they call dropper seatposts which allow you to raise and lower the height of the seat on your bike for various riding conditions. When you are climbing hills, you want the seat up high to get the full range of motion from your legs, and when going downhill, you want the seat low so the seat and seatpost are out of your way for when you need to lean back or take turns at a high rate of speed. Before dropper seatposts, you would have to stop and manually raise and lower your seatpost as needed or just suffer with it in one position for the entire ride. (Try riding down a steep hill with your seat up and let me know how that feels!)

When these dropper seatposts came out, they were kind of primitive, and many only had certain positions you could put the seat at. Now they are made so that you can put them at exactly the height you desire at any time while riding. For the most part, they are mechanically actuated, but there are a few models that use hydraulic fluid like your brakes do.

You will have a cable that runs from the seatpost itself to your handlebars, which will then have a lever attached to it. You use this lever to make the seatpost go up and down as needed. To make it go up, simply stand up on your pedals and press the lever and it will pop up automatically. To make it go down, hold down the lever while sitting on the seat and use your weight to push it down. If you don't want it to go down all the way, simply release the lever at the point where you want it to stop. This works the same while making the seat go up.

Seatpost Shaft

Most seatposts these days use hidden cable routing where the cable is connected to the bottom of the seatpost, run through the frame, then out a hole in the frame, and then to the lever mounted on the handlebars. Older models will have the cable coming out near the top of the seatpost and then run alongside the frame of the bike. There are also wireless seatposts that don't require any cabling yet they will require a rechargeable battery to keep them working. You can usually go several months between charges.

These seatposts come in various lengths as well, ranging from 125mm up to 240mm, and you need to get the right size for your height. If you get a seatpost that is too short for you, then you will need to raise it higher out of the frame, which will not allow it to go down as far in the lowest position. If you look at the picture above, you will see that the seatpost is sticking out quite a bit from the frame, and the shaft is the part that goes up and down while the rest will stay in a fixed position.

Chapter 7 – Proper Eating and Hydration

One thing you will soon discover once you start doing some serious riding or riding in the heat is that you need to keep your food and liquid intake going, otherwise you are asking for trouble. Mountain biking takes some serious energy, and you need to keep your body fueled, otherwise it will start giving up on you and this is not a good thing when you are miles away from home.

I have been in situations where I didn't bring enough food or water and it can make it impossible to go on, especially when you have climbing to do. Even if it's all downhill, if you don't have your energy level up, then you won't be on your game and you will find yourself riding sloppily down the hill, which can result in a crash.

There are several ways to keep your energy and hydration up to speed while on the trail, and it's not that difficult to eat and drink what you need to keep you going. In this chapter, I will discuss what you will need to bring with you on the trail, and how you should prepare before hitting the trail.

How Often to Eat and Drink

It's not only a matter of what to eat and drink during your rides but also how often to eat and drink. The type of riding your do plus the condition that you are in will affect how often you need to keep the fuel supply going, but it's always better to overdo it a little than not do it enough. When it comes to keeping your energy level up, a lack of water can make you feel like you're running out of steam.

It's always a good idea to eat something before your ride so you have some fuel to work with. This doesn't necessarily mean a cheeseburger and fries, but rather something a little healthier that contains some calories, protein, and carbohydrates. Also, try not to eat right before the ride starts, because you could end up with some cramps. Give yourself a half hour or so before hitting the trail.

The same thing applies to water. Try to avoid coffee and energy drinks because they contain caffeine, which actually dehydrates you. Stick with either water for breakfast or maybe something like orange juice or some other kind of juice. If I know I'm going on a long, hot ride, then I will drink a bottle of Gatorade or something similar before the ride to help get myself ready.

Always be sure to take snack breaks while riding, because you don't want to push yourself too far and then try to recover with food after you are already exhausted. Even if you are not hungry, you can eat a few chews or half of a protein bar just to get that energy regenerating as you ride.

Proper Amount of Water

Everyone knows you need to stay hydrated while exercising, but how much water do you really need? Well, this will vary depending on the temperature you are riding in, how far you are riding, and what kind of shape you are in.

It's always better to take too much water than not enough. If you are planning on a long ride, you might want to take a hydration pack since it can hold more water than a bottle that you would put in your bottle cage. And if you are really going far or it's a really hot day, then you can certainly use both. The only downside is the extra weight, but as you ride, you will be lightening your load while you drink it.

Whether you are thirsty or not, you should be drinking your water as you ride. You should try and drink about 20 ounces per hour on your ride. Most water bottles are around 20-25 ounces, so that means one bottle per hour. A typical hydration pack holds around 75-100 ounces of water. If it's a cool day and you are just taking an easy stroll with no real elevation gain, then you can taper that down a little bit.

After the ride, you should always drink some water to recover what you have lost and maybe even a sports drink to get some electrolytes back in your system. If it was a tough workout, then you may find yourself thirsty for the rest of the day, so keep the water intake going.

Electrolyte Drinks\Tablets

Many people (including myself) take advantage of the many electrolyte drinks out there so that you can keep your muscles and nerves functioning properly during and after exercising. When you sweat, you lose electrolytes and fluids. Your muscles need these to function properly and your kidneys need them to keep filtering out the bad stuff inside you that needs to be let out.

Drinks like Gatorade put back the electrolytes and sodium your body loses while sweating it out on the trail. Most of these drinks also contain glucose (sugar) that your body needs to recover as well. Overall, it's just a faster way to let your body recover rather than waiting for water and food to do their thing. These drinks will have their share of calories as well, so if you are on a weight loss plan then keep that in mind.

You can also get electrolyte tablets that you can put in your water bottle and drink throughout the ride. They come in a variety of flavors and dissolve in water very quickly. I actually had an issue with being lightheaded after rides, and then I started using these tablets and the problem is pretty much gone now. You can get these tablets at many bike shops or online if you want to give them a shot. You can get a tube of around twelve of them for $6 or so.

Gels and Chews

Gels have been around for a long time and are commonly used when doing longer distance rides where you need some recovery while out on the trail. These gels contain maltodextrin, fructose, electrolytes, and amino acids that help muscle recovery and give you a boost of energy at the same time. Some of them even come with caffeine for an extra jolt.

There are many brands and flavors to choose from, and some people like certain brands over others. You can simply go to a bike shop and buy individual packets and try them out for yourself. For most of them, you should drink some water after using them, while others don't require you to do so.

Chews are an alternative to gels and offer similar benefits while being more filling at the same time. They also come in a variety of flavors and there are many brands to choose from. You can even get organic chews if you are the type who usually likes to stay more natural.

I will usually take a pouch of chews on most rides in case I get hungry and then take both for longer rides. I try to stick with one gel every couple of miles when climbing.

Bars
Energy or protein bars are another good food source that you can take with you on the trail. They are easy to carry and easy to digest (assuming you get the right ones and don't

end up with a glorified candy bar full of sugar and empty calories). If you choose a bar that is less appealing, then that probably means it's better for you and will have the things you are looking for!

When doing long rides, it's a good idea to bring a couple of bars since you will get hungry, and if you don't feed your body it will start slowing down fast. Even if you aren't really hungry, it's a good idea to eat one if it's been a while since you last ate something. This way you don't need to worry about actually getting hungry and running out of fuel too soon. These bars usually contain many vitamins and minerals without too much sugar to go along with them. They usually contain a good amount of carbohydrates as well.

I really like the waffle wafer type snacks since they are light and easy to eat and taste really good. There are a few companies that make that sort of thing.

Fruit & Nuts

If you really want to treat your body right on your rides, then look into bringing some nuts and fruits along with you. Sure it's not as easy as putting a couple of gels and an energy bar in your pocket or backpack, but if you choose the right types of nuts and fruits, you can pull it off.

Bananas are great to eat while exercising because they contain potassium, magnesium, and useful carbohydrates. Plus they are generally light and won't make you feel bogged down after you eat them. The downside is that they take up room in your pack, and it's not something you can just stick in your pocket.

Oranges and tangerines are another good fruit to eat while riding. The skin prevents them from making a mess of your pack, and since it's biodegradable you don't have to feel too bad if you don't have a trash can and have to toss the peel in the bushes. The downside is that they can be messy to eat. Apples are another fruit to consider.

Dehydrated\dried fruits like apricots and dates can also be a good trail food. Just be careful not to overdo it because these fruits can contain a lot of sugar, and it's easy to eat an entire bag in one sitting!

Nuts are a great trail food because they are easy to carry, don't make a mess, are filling, and provide you with usable energy without a lot of the bad stuff you don't want. Try to stay away from salted or roasted nuts because they will just make you thirsty and are not as nutritious.

There are many nuts you can eat while out on the trail, and here is a list of some of the best ones:

- Almonds
- Pistachios
- Walnuts
- Macadamia
- Peanuts
- Pecans
- Hazelnuts
- Brazil Nuts

Trail mix is another great snack because it comes with a variety of nuts and also things like raisins or other dried fruits. I like to get the type with M&Ms mixed in to get my chocolate fix!

Other Helpful Foods

One problem with making sure you keep yourself fed while out on the trail is that some of these snacks that are good for you can kind of be on the bland side, and there are other options if you want something a little more exciting.

Beef jerky is a great choice for a quick snack, and everyone likes beef jerky (well, except for vegetarians, of course). It's easy to carry and has the protein your muscles need to recover. It's also a great snack to eat after a ride. If you don't like beef jerky, you can always try some turkey jerky. There may even be tofu jerky out there for the non-meat eaters!

Another great on-the-trail snack is an old favorite: a peanut butter and jelly sandwich. These are great to eat before a ride, and you can also bring them with you in your pack since they can last a while before you have to eat them. Peanut butter has protein, the jelly will give you a sugar boost, and the bread has some carbs to refill your tank.

Protein shakes are another thing you can drink to give your body what it needs before a ride. Obviously, you can't take it with you unless you put it in your water bottle, but that wouldn't work out too well. You can make protein shakes with things like fruit and yogurt, or just your basic off the shelf protein powder. On a side note, chocolate milk is also a great drink for recovery after your ride.

Chapter 8 – Improving Your Riding Skills

In order to become a well-rounded mountain biker that can take on any type of terrain, it's going to take a bit of practice. Also, the better you take care of yourself, the better you will be able to ride. Whatever you do, don't expect it to happen overnight!

There are many aspects to mountain biking that you can work on to improve your overall riding ability. If you plan on riding various types of trails and also venturing off into unknown territory, it's a good idea to be a well-rounded rider so you don't have to worry about getting stuck on a trail that might be out of your comfort zone. When you are worried about crashing, that is usually the time that you will crash.

Stretching and Working Out

Being in good physical shape will really help you out when it comes to tackling difficult and challenging terrain. One thing you will notice is that the smaller, skinny guys (and gals) are the ones who seem to be able to ride over anything like it's nothing. Weight makes a big difference when it comes to riding, and even if you are 200 lbs. of solid muscle, it's still not the same as 150 lbs. of lean riding machine. Think of it as having a bike that weighs 50 lbs. more than the other guy. You will need to carry that weight around with you, which can take its toll when climbing those hills.

Having strong legs is also a bonus since that is what you use to move you along the trail. You don't need to have calves the size of grapefruits but having some good overall strength in your legs will help out quite a bit. If you go to the gym, then you can work them out on the various leg machines to get all of those muscles moving that you might normally not use too much. Of course, riding will build your leg muscles as well, but doing some weight training will also give you an advantage.

There is an ongoing debate about whether you should stretch before going on your ride. Some say you should, while others say you shouldn't because your muscles are cold and you risk overextending or pulling something. I usually don't before a ride, and never have any problems. A friend of mine made a good point when he said: *"Do animals out in the wild stretch before going after their prey?"*

I think you are better off stretching *after* your ride since your muscles are warmed up and probably in need of some attention. What you can do before a ride instead is something like jumping jacks to get the blood flowing and get your muscles warmed up.

Climbing

One of the most challenging things for new riders is climbing up hills without wanting to throw up or give up. If you are out of shape, then hill climbs will be brutal and will zap your motivation really quickly. Even if you are in shape, mountain biking is not the same as other activities such as running or swimming, so just because you do another sport, it doesn't mean you will be an expert climber.

Start with short hills that do not have a lot of incline and make sure your bike is set up properly so you are in the correct riding position to properly climb those hills. You will need to be the correct height on the seat, and also the correct distance from the handlebars. I mentioned earlier in the book how longer stems will make climbing easier, so if you find that you are doing wheelies or that the front end wants to constantly lift off the ground, then you might want to check your stem length. A good stem length to start with is around 60-70mm for more cross country style riding and maybe 50-60mm for more technical or steeper trails. You wouldn't think 10mm would make a difference but it really does!

Also, make sure your gearing is good for climbing and that you have a low enough (granny) gear, otherwise you will really be struggling on your climbs. The chainring size up front will make a difference too and is easier to change than the cassette in the rear, so you might want to go a little smaller to help out on the climbs if you are having trouble. Just count the number of teeth on the chainring to see what size it is and take it from there.

Downhill

You might think that going downhill is easier than going uphill because of the obvious lack of pedaling. Sure, physically it can be easier, but it's still something you need to be good at to be a serious mountain biker. And when you get into some serious downhill riding, you will find that it can be just as exhausting as going uphill.

Obviously, you are going faster when going downhill, so you need to be aware of your surroundings and know what's coming up. One of the biggest mistakes that many mountain bikers do is look down at the ground in front of them rather than the trail ahead of them. If you are looking down at the trail in front of your front tire, then by the time you see the rock, root, rut, rabbit, or whatever it is in front of you, it's too late to react properly. This even applies to going uphill and will make your riding smoother overall. Proper bike\stance position makes a difference as well, so if you are going down something steep, you should be leaning back on your bike to apply more weight to the rear to avoid putting your weight over the handlebars and maybe even going over them! Also be sure to put your seat down on your dropper post so it's not in your way when leaning back. Some people will ride downhill with their seat up, but if you try it both ways, you will what kind of a difference it makes with the seat down.

For the most part, you want to unlock your suspension when going downhill unless it's something that is super smooth or not too fast or steep. Your suspension will absorb the bumps and rocks and help to keep you in control at speed.

Also be aware of your braking when it comes to the front and rear brakes. Using just the rear will not allow you to slow down as fast and force you to use more braking power to slow down, which might end up making the rear wheel lock up and slide (which will be harder to control). Too much front braking will make you nose heavy and force your body forward over the handlebars. After a while, you will get the feel of how much front and rear brake to use to balance things out.

Jumps and Drops
Now here is where things get tricky. I don't advise trying jumps or drops until you have a higher level of bike control, otherwise you are simply asking for trouble. If you don't have any bike control, you are just going to fly in the direction you were heading when you hit the jump and be hoping for the best for the landing. If you really need to jump off of something, stick to the curb in the beginning.

You might have noticed on those videos you have been watching that the riders look like they are steering the bike in the air to make it go where they want to land. That is what I mean by bike control, and no, you don't need to be able to jump like the pros to be able to jump at all, but you need to start off slow. Don't go for any type of jump that has a rough landing or requires you to clear an obstacle or pit to make it to the other side.

If you find a nice jump with a smooth landing, then do it over and over again until it seems effortless, then move on to something bigger. You might want to try going to a bike park and taking one of the easy runs to get the hang of things since they are designed to be easier to ride and not have any death traps on them.

When jumping, make sure your seat is down, your feet are flat with the pedals level, and your arms are out and a little bent at the elbows. Some people like to squeeze their seat with their legs for a little more stability. Once again, keep your eyes ahead of you and not down in front of you, and always know a way out if you change your mind. On some jumps, slowing down at the last minute will cause you to have an undesirable result. And, most importantly, scope out the jump before you try it.

For drops, you will need to make sure you have the right approach speed and also lean back and pull up on the handlebars to some degree so you don't nosedive off the drop. You want to land with both wheels hitting the ground at about the same time. If anything, I would let the back land before the front if possible.

If you change your mind at the last minute and can't slow down enough to stop, then try and pull the front end up to land on your rear tire rather than going front wheel first over the drop. For smaller drops, you will be ok because your suspension will absorb the impact, but for larger drops, you will probably be going over the bars if you go too slow. Once again, make sure your suspension is unlocked to absorb the impact.

Rock Gardens
Rock gardens can be tricky, and the terrain makes a difference in how you should ride them. For many riders, this can be a deal breaker when it comes to certain trails because they don't feel confident when riding in those kinds of conditions, which is understandable (especially for beginners).

But once you tackle your fear of riding rocky trails, you may actually begin to enjoy them and start seeking them out! Rocky terrain can be some of the most challenging and fun type of riding you can do because it tests your balance, skill, and guts. I'm sure you have seen those YouTube videos of the riders flying down rocky hillsides like they didn't even know the rocks were there.

Riding style comes into play on rocky trails, as does the way you actually ride them. When going over larger rocks or down rocky hills, you want to make sure you are leaning back to avoid going over the bars and to keep yourself balanced. It's also a good idea to keep your seat down so when you are leaning back, you don't get caught up on it. Another thing that helps is to keep your speed up over the rocks. This may not seem like a good idea while you are about to ride over some, but it helps you to keep your balance and actually smooths out the ride. Just keep in mind that this only applies to rocks that are a certain size, and most likely won't help you over large boulders. Once you get comfortable, you can start jumping off and over the rocks when you get to them to add some excitement to the ride.

Tire pressure is also another important factor for these types of trails. You are more prone to getting flats on rocky trails than on smoother ones. There is some debate about running lower or higher pressure over rocks, but we tend to say stick on the high side. Running higher pressure will help prevent pinch flats, which is when the tire gets pinched on a rock and punctures the tube. Running higher pressure will make the ride bouncier and give you less traction, but it may be better than changing your tube five times on a ride. By higher pressure, we are referring to the mid to upper 30s when it comes to psi, but you may want to play with some different pressures to see what works best for you.

Finally, you should make sure that you are wearing the proper protection for these more difficult types of trails. When you take a fall on rocks, it hurts more than it does on a nice smooth trail. Your protection options include a full face helmet if you are going more hardcore, elbow pads, and knee pads. You can get flexible elbow and knee pads that are more comfortable and can be worn for longer periods of time without getting in the way compared to pads that have plastic inserts\cups inside them.

Cornering

Taking corners can be harder than you would think, and it is one of the things that many riders need to focus on. If you are just cruising along at a slow pace, then it's not a problem because you simply turn into the corners and everything is usually fine.

When you get into high speed cornering, that is where things get more complicated. When taking corners at speed, you want to lean into them more than you want to steer into them. That is why the tires you generally put in the front of your bike will have knobbies on the edge that will give you grip when leaning the bike into a turn.

If you turn the handlebars rather than lean into a turn, then you don't get to use this part of the tire, which can result in the front end of the bike washing out and losing control. Of course, the type of dirt you are riding on will make a big difference. If it's a sandy surface or loose rocks, then you will be looking at some extra effort (and skill) to keep your bike in control during cornering.

When taking turns at speed, try to keep your feet level with the ground in comparison to the cranks. You will also want to keep some bend in your elbows and knees, which will allow you to move the bike along with the terrain. Also, try to shift your weight onto the pedal on the outside of the turn for more grip and to keep the inside pedal from hitting the ground when leaning into a turn.

Bikes with shorter stems will generally handle better, especially with some wider bars to give you that extra leverage. This is because today's bikes are slacker than ever, meaning the front tire is out further in front of you compared to a few years ago.

I know you heard me say this before, but I will say it again. *Look ahead on the trail, focus on where you want to go, and watch for the entrance and exit points of the turn.* You also want to make sure you brake *before* you get to the corner, not while you're *in* the corner. This is the same thing race car drivers do around corners, and it applies to bikes as well.

Nothing will slow you down more than coming into a corner too fast and then having to slam on the brakes to avoid going off the trail. If you do this, then you will have no speed left for when you exit the corner. Also, try to get in the gear you want before the corner so you are not stuck shifting while pedaling out of it.

Strava and Trailforks

One way to improve your skills is to track your rides and compare your performance to how it was at other times you rode the same trail. It can be hard to tell if your performance is improving because sometimes you can feel fast when you were slow and sometimes things feel slow but were actually fast. Being able to see your past performance statistics on the same trail can really shed some light on your progress.

Using a smartphone and a performance tracking app can help you see how you are progressing, and it's also a fun way to compare yourself with others on the same trail. Strava is one of the top apps used for this type of thing, and it's free to use for Android and iPhone. They do have a pay for version with additional features, but the free version gives you plenty of information to work with.

I have included some screenshots from the Strava app below, and you can also view your stats from the Strava website and get additional information about your rides. As you can see, once you complete a ride and save it, you will be shown information such as the total distance, elevation gain, moving time, and average speed.

You can then go into the Analysis section and see things such as your speed and elevation gain throughout the duration of the ride.

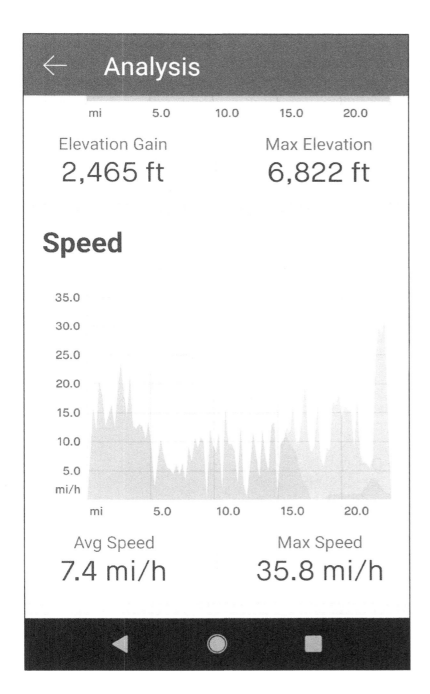

Each ride will have segments that have been created by Strava users throughout the years. You can even create your own segments if there is a trail you ride that is not on the Strava app. (The segment lengths and names will vary depending on where you ride.) Once you are done with your ride, you will see the total number of segments and also your achievements. Achievements are only shown when you have done a segment more than once and have done it faster than you have in previous attempts. Strava will show a gold medal with a PR on it designating a personal record and will also show when you have your second and third fastest times.

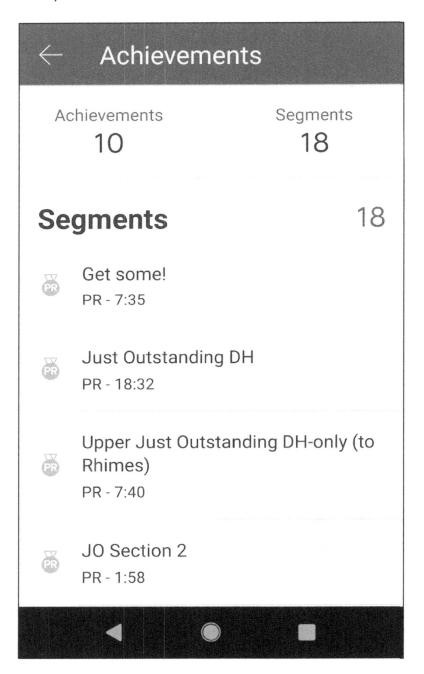

Going into a segment's details will show you how you did compared to others and compared to yourself. You will see your all-time rank, and if you go into it, it will show you how you rank compared to everyone who has done that trail and uses Strava. Tapping on Your Results will show you all of your recorded times so you can see how fast you were on what date.

Strava allows you to follow your friends and other people so you can see where they are riding and how they compare to you performance wise. Tapping on Following will show you how you rank in comparison to everyone you follow.

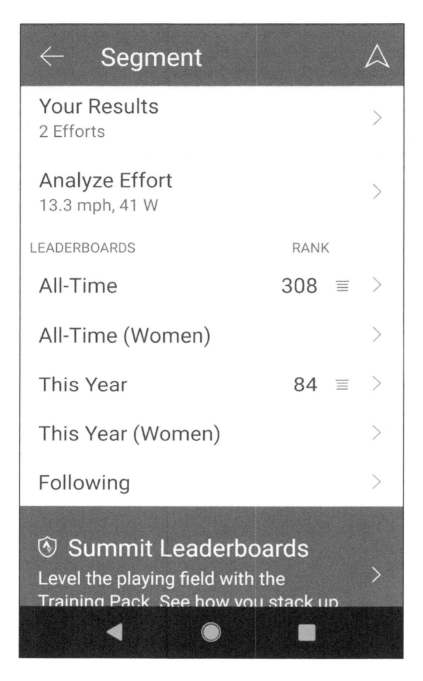

You can also view your ride on a map and have certain segments highlighted so you know where that segment was located.

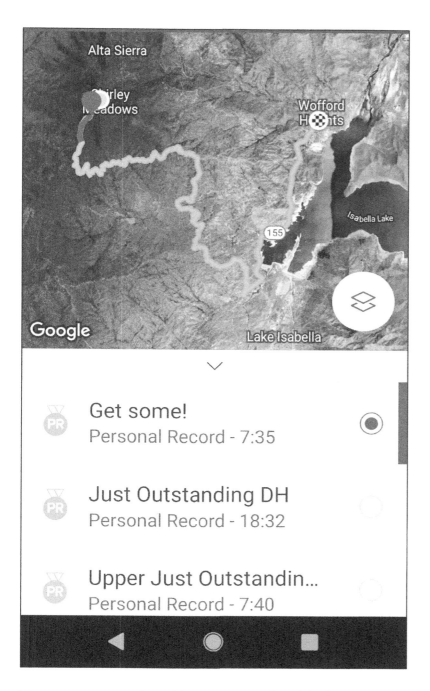

There are many other things you can do with the Strava app and on the Strava website, so sign up for free and give it a shot. They also have a pay for subscription plan that offers many additional features.

Trailforks is another app and website I recommend because it's created by riders who map out the trails usually using Strava data, and then you can do things like post updates, add photos and videos, and give reports. You can view trails for just about any location and get details on the specific trails themselves.

I like to use it to find new trails in my area that I have not ridden, plus I can find out details about the trails before riding them. You can see things such as elevation gain and loss, difficulty ratings, and descriptions of the trails themselves.

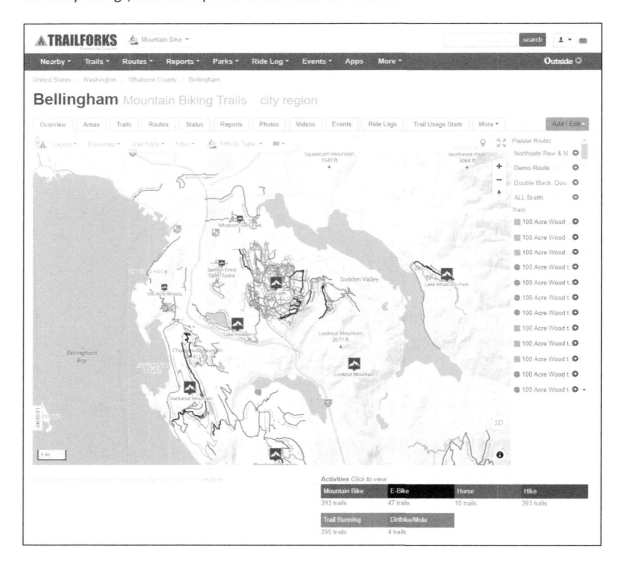

Once you zoom into the area you want to ride in, then all the trails will show up and you can see their ratings based on their colors (like discussed in Chapter 2). You will also be shown a listing of the trails in the area and be given stats for that area.

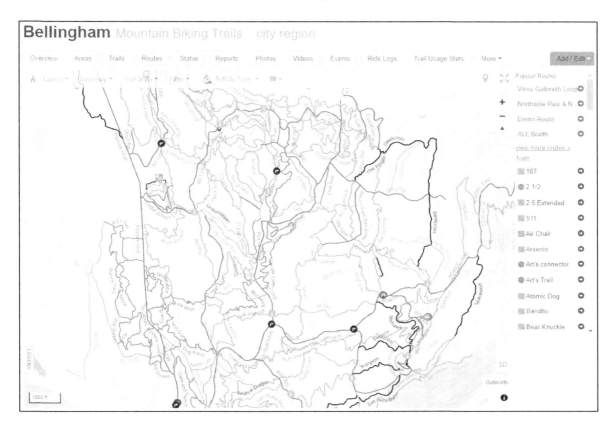

Clicking on a specific trail will bring up its details and show you all kinds of information, as well as any videos or photos that were uploaded by Trailforks users.

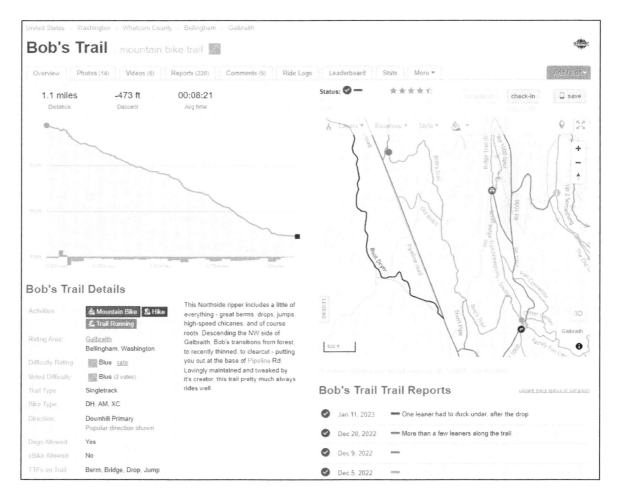

The smartphone app comes in very handy when you are out on the trail and are trying to figure out where you are and what trails are around you.

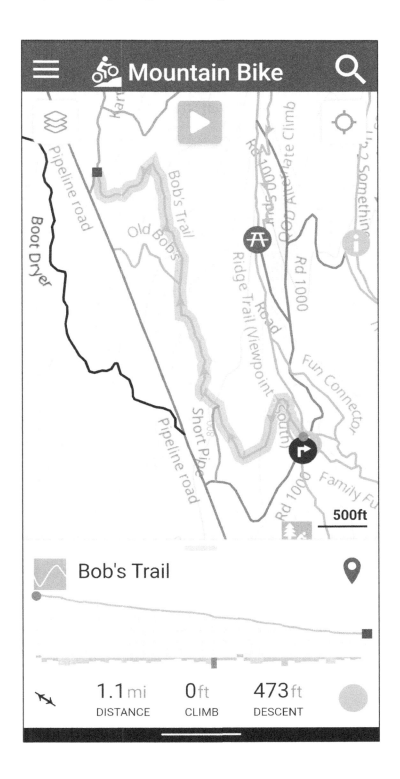

You can join the site for free and add trails, videos, pictures, and reports to contribute to the Trailforks community. They do require you to subscribe for a small monthly fee to gain access to all the trails outside of your local area. You can even have it import your Strava data to get additional reports that you can't get from Strava itself.

Chapter 9 – Bike Maintenance

Owning a bike is similar to owning a car when it comes to maintenance. If you don't keep your equipment up to par, then it will start to give out on you and not perform at its best. A mountain bike is not as expensive to maintain as a car, but you do need to do maintenance a lot more often.

There are a few things you should be doing before every ride as well as things you should do on a schedule or as they become necessary to do. Even if you choose not to do the harder stuff on your own, you should still plan on bringing your bike into your local shop for maintenance as required.

General Maintenance
There are quite a few things you should be doing on a regular basis to keep your bike operating at its best. Some of these things should be done before each ride or at least before every couple of rides, and they really don't take too much time to do.

Lubrication is one of the things you should be doing every ride or two because without proper lubrication, things get noisy and don't work so well. For the most part, you only need to worry about your chain, even though there are other parts of your bike that require lubrication to work properly, just not on a regular basis. There are many upon many brands of chain lube on the market, and it's impossible to find the best one, so once you find one that works, stick with it. There are chain lubes for wet conditions, dry conditions, dusty conditions, and so on. Plus, they are made with different ingredients (such as wax, etc.), so it can be enough to make your head spin.

Checking your tire pressure is a must as well since it can have a dramatic effect on how your bike performs. (I will be getting into more detail on tire pressure in the next section.)

Cleaning your bike is not a requirement, but if you like to take care of your stuff, then it's something you should do. There are specialty cleaners for your drivetrain as well as things like the frame itself. I am a fan of White Lightning Bike Wash for general frame cleaning and Finish Line Super Bike Wash for the drivetrain. If you ride in muddy conditions, it's best to just let it dry and then use a brush kit to brush all the dirt away rather than hosing your bike down. If you are always hosing it down, then you risk getting water into places where it shouldn't and causing corrosion or breaking down grease that is there to keep things moving smoothly. One good thing about cleaning your bike is it allows you to spot problems that you might not see because they are covered over with dirt or because you are not looking closely at your bike like you do when you're cleaning it.

One other thing you should do on a regular basis is check the tightness of all the bolts on your bike. Since mountain bikes get rattled around constantly on the trail, sometimes things can come loose, and you definitely don't want your bike coming apart or something falling off while flying down a hill.

Check things like the pivot point bolts, seatpost, handlebar stem, and wheel axles to make sure everything is snug. Whatever you do, don't go *overtightening* things, because most of these bolts have torque specs that they should be tightened to.

Tires

Many people check their tire pressure before every ride, and if you are the type that likes an exact pressure in your tires, then you might want to do this yourself. Just because you put air in your tires doesn't mean it will stay exactly the same pressure forever. It only takes a couple of minutes to check the pressure, and then a couple more minutes to add air. Plus, if you notice that the pressure is really low and you just rode your bike the other day, that may indicate that you have a leak in your tire.

I mentioned tire pressure gauges in Chapter 5, and the one on your floor pump might not be too accurate, so it's a good idea to get a dedicated gauge. They are small, cheap, and easy to take with you if needed.

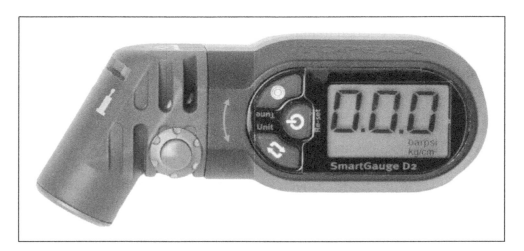

Once you find a tire pressure that works best for your style of riding and the trails that you normally ride on, then it will be easy to keep your tires inflated properly to get the best performance out of them.

You should also keep an eye on your tires for signs of wear. The rear tire will usually wear faster than the front tire since many people tend to lock up the rear brakes and slide around corners or over rocks. Once the tire gets too worn, then you will have issues with traction when stopping as well as climbing. When the front tire gets too worn, you will have handling issues.

When bike tires get too old, they will start to dry out, and the knobbies will wear and even break off. Most people will wear out their tires before they get too old, but you should still check the general overall condition of your tires. The same thing goes for inner tubes. They can get old as well, but you will most likely replace them from punctures before having to worry about them getting too old. (Unless you patch them over and over again for a long time.)

If you go the tubeless route in your tires, you will need to replace or add more sealant at regular intervals. The sealant in the tires only lasts a few months before it starts to dry out and needs to either be cleaned out and replaced, or you can add some more to the tire. I like to add more sealant every three to four months and then clean it out the next time so I don't have a large buildup of dried up sealant. (I will be going over tubeless tire setup in the next chapter.)

Suspension Maintenance and Care
Your shock and fork also require periodic maintenance to keep them performing at their best. If you don't do this, then your ride quality will suffer because the suspension won't be doing its job properly.

Fork manufacturers have specifications on when you should service a fork. Generally it is every thirty hours or so of riding. You might think that is excessive, but it will also depend on the type of riding you are doing. A basic service includes replacing the oil in the fork and checking all the seals for wear and damage. A more intensive service will include replacing the seals as well as the oil and can be done after a longer interval such as 100 hours or so.

As for general maintenance, you should always clean the stanchions and the seals located at the top end of the fork lower to ensure that dirt is not getting past the seal and contaminating the oil and internal seals. I like to use an old toothbrush to get in there and clean all the dirt out. Old toothbrushes work great for other bike cleaning tasks as well. Also check the stanchions for scratches that might damage seals when the stanchion moves in and out of the lower.

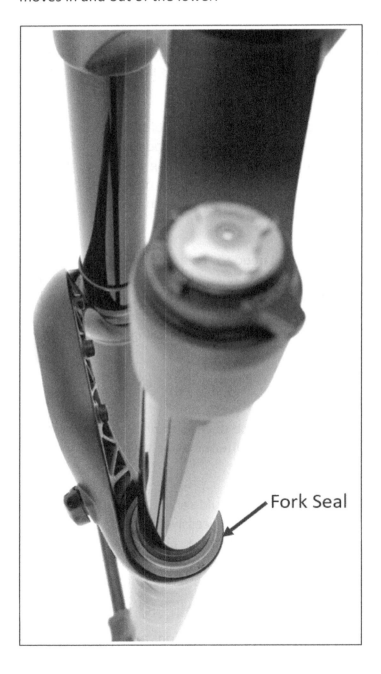

Fork Seal

Unless you are mechanically inclined, you might want to have this service done by a professional at a bike shop, or at least find good instructions or a video before tackling it yourself. A basic service might cost around $60 while a full service can be double that.

Although not as complex, rear shocks need to be serviced as well, although not as often. For example, the shock on one of my bikes says the service interval is 200 hours, which is much less frequent than a fork service. Shock service will not cost as much either.

Another thing that you need to do periodically is check your fork and shock air pressure. The bike manufacturer should provide the recommended air pressure for both based on your weight. This doesn't mean you have to stick with their recommendation, but it's a good place to start. Once you get the pressure setting that works for you, then you should check every couple of weeks to make sure that you still have that amount of air pressure in your suspension. If it drops drastically, then that means you have an issue and should take it in for a service.

Brake Pad Replacement & Bleeding

Brake pads will wear out on your bike just like they do on your car, so they need to be replaced before they get too far worn down and then damage the rotors. I mentioned in Chapter 6 that when the thickness of the pads gets down to about that of a dime then it's time to replace them. Brake pads are fairly easy to replace, and the method varies depending on the make and model of your brakes. Just be sure not to get any contaminants on your new brake pads, otherwise you will end up with squeaky brakes that don't work as well as they should.

Replacing the pads is just a matter of removing the wheel and any bolt that is holding in the existing pads. I like to level out the brake lever and crack the bleed screw on the reservoir just a tiny bit. Then I will use a large flathead screwdriver and push on the old pads while still in the caliper to push the pistons back in. Whatever you do, don't do this with the new pads or on the pistons themselves.

Then I will slide in the new pads and bolt them down, tighten the bleed screw, and put the wheel back on. Don't forget to reposition your brake lever if you moved it to level it. Next, spin the wheel and see if the rotor is rubbing on the new pads. If so, then you will need to loosen the caliper bolts a little and try and get them centered on the rotor all the way around it. This is a trial and error type of thing, but you will get better at it the more you do it.

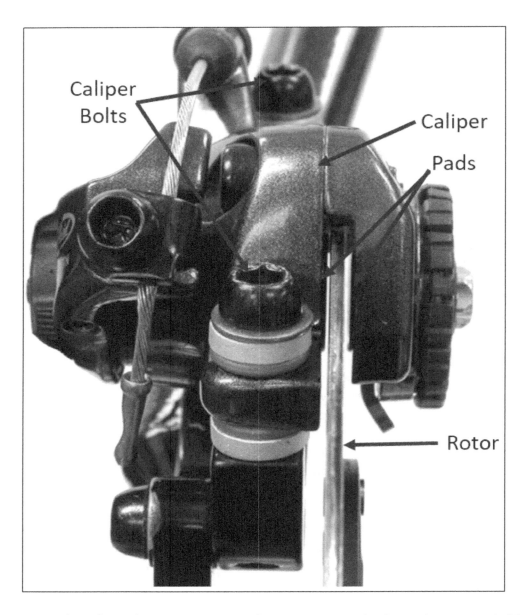

One other thing that is important when it comes to brake maintenance is bleeding your brakes. Occasionally you might find that the brake lever is feeling soft, or you have to squeeze it many times to "pump up" the brakes to make them work correctly. This is because air got in the lines that are used to move the hydraulic fluid that makes the brakes work. This can happen if you open the brake system for any reason, or if you have a damaged brake line or seal that is letting air into the system.

Bleeding the brakes clears any air out of the lines so that the brakes will work the way they are supposed to. The method for bleeding brakes varies between brands and models, but the concept is the same. What you are doing is attaching a syringe at each end of the brake system; so you will have one on the brake lever and one on the caliper, and each of these will have a bleed screw that you can remove to attach the special syringe into. From there you are injecting brake fluid in one side while forcing it out the other side to remove any air from the system.

Brake bleed kits will vary depending on what brakes you have, so make sure you get the type that will work for your brakes. A good kit will have everything you need to get the job done.

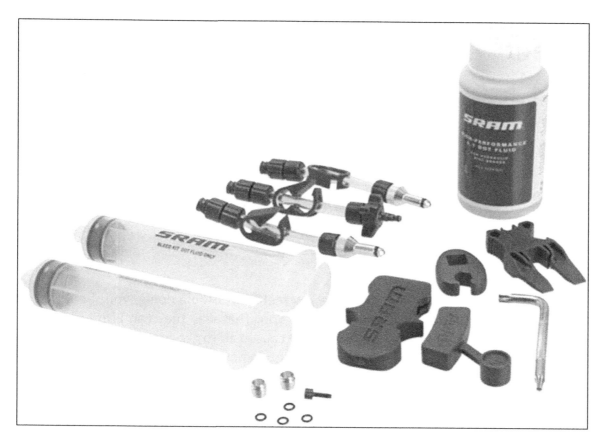

One important thing is to make sure you use the correct type of fluid for your brakes. Most brakes either use a DOT fluid (like your car does) or mineral oil. Here is a list of some of the more common brake manufacturers and fluid types they use.

Manufacturer	Mineral Oil	DOT Fluid
Avid		✔
Formula		✔
Giant	✔	✔
Hayes		✔
Hope		✔
Magura	✔	
Shimano	✔	

If bleeding your brakes is not something you feel comfortable doing, you should take it into your local shop and have them do it for you. That way they can also inspect your brake system to see if there are any issues that caused air to get into the lines. Most shops charge around $20 per side for brake bleeding. Sometimes it's good to do a complete brake fluid flush to get the old fluid out of the system and replace it with fresh fluid since it will eventually break down.

Drivetrain
In order to keep your bike shifting and pedaling smoothly, you will need to do regular drivetrain maintenance on the various components that make up the drivetrain. Mountain bikes are made to take a beating and get dirty, but the drivetrain needs to be cleaned and lubricated more often than any other part of the bike. I discussed the

drivetrain components in Chapter 6, but to refresh your memory, here is a picture of the drivetrain components.

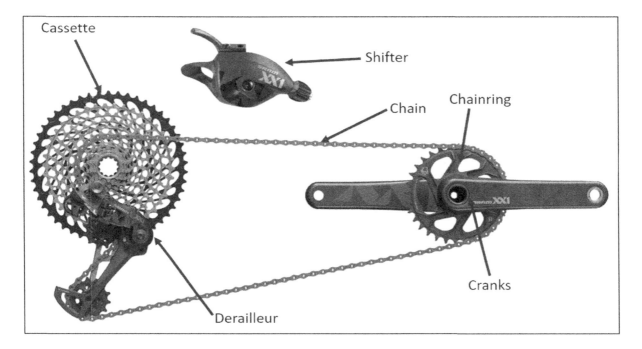

Now I will break down what drivetrain maintenance consists of and what you need to do in regard to each component.

- **Shifters** – The shifters on your bike generally do not require any maintenance unless you break something in a crash etc. They usually last forever and are pretty durable.

- **Derailleur** – The derailleur is responsible for shifting gears by moving the chain to the different size rings on the rear cassette when you push or pull on the shifter lever. For the most part, it's a set it and forget it type situation, but if your bike becomes hard to shift, won't stay in gear, or starts shifting on its own, then it's time for an adjustment. Derailleur adjusting can be tricky, and if you don't know what you are doing, then you can actually make it shift worse than before you started, so it might be a good idea to leave it to the pros. Another reason your bike might have shifting issues is from a stretched out or broken shifter cable. These cables don't last forever, and eventually need to be replaced.

As for derailleur maintenance, just be sure to keep it clean and remove any grime from the jockey wheels to keep the chain moving freely. The jockey wheels can get dirty from getting oil from the chain on them and then having dirt stick to that oil. I like to use an old toothbrush to keep them clean.

Jockey Wheels

- **Chainring** – The chainring is the front ring connected to the cranks and is what is used to connect to the rear cassette via the chain. These don't require much maintenance except for keeping the teeth clean like you do with the jockey wheels on the derailleur. The chainring will eventually wear out because the teeth will wear down, and it may cause things like noise or even the chain slipping if it's really bad. It can also be damaged by hitting rocks etc., so check it over and look for any bent or broken teeth.

- **Cassette** – Cassette maintenance is similar to chainring maintenance, and it's mostly about keeping it clean and checking for damage. You can clean your cassette with some drivetrain cleaner and a brush, or even a toothbrush. There are even brushes designed for cleaning cassettes.

- **Chain** – Cleaning your chain is one of those things you should be doing on a regular basis since it can get dirty very quickly and is running through your chainring and cassette, transferring dirt as it goes. You can use the same cleaner you use on your other drivetrain components or get some dedicated chain cleaner and run your chain through a rag while pedaling the bike on a stand or backpedaling it on the ground.

  There are also dedicated chain cleaning tools where you put a cleaning solvent in the tool (which contains brushes), and then you run the chain through the tool itself. You don't need to use one of these every time you clean your chain, but it's a good idea to do this every couple of months (unless you ride in very dirty conditions).

- **Cranks** – Cranks themselves generally don't require any maintenance except making sure they are not damaged or that the bolts are not loose. Many people will put crank boots on the ends of the crank arms to protect them from rock strikes. I recommend using these, especially if you have carbon cranks.

Another component related to the cranks is called the bottom bracket. The bottom bracket is a set of bearings that is installed inside the frame's bottom bracket shell. It is the interface for the crankset and the frame and secures the cranks so they don't move around within the frame. There are bearings inside of the bottom bracket that help the cranks spin smoothly inside the frame. Bottom brackets come as either threaded or press-fit types.

The bottom brackets do occasionally need to be cleaned and re-greased to keep them operating at their best. They will also wear out eventually and need to be replaced. It's not a difficult job if you have the tools to do so. Just be sure to get the right type to match the one you are replacing. Most bike shops should be able to get you what you need based on the make and model of your bike.

Chapter 10 – Upgrading Your Bike

Just like with many things in our lives, there is always room for improvement, and your mountain bike is no different. Bike manufacturers try and configure bikes so they work the best for the greatest amount of people, and you might or might not fall into that category.

Once you get a bike, you may find that certain areas need improvement or can be better, and then the upgrade process begins. Then, before you know it, your bike is worth twice as much as you paid for it because you just couldn't stop making it better! In this chapter I will go over what you can do to upgrade your bike, and if it's really worth doing so.

Is it Worth it?

The simple answer to this question is yes, it is worth it. As you get better at riding, you will benefit from a bike that can keep up with the way you ride. Imagine taking a cross county bike on a downhill course. Sure it can be done, but it definitely won't be a smooth ride, and you sure won't be having any fun because the bike is not suited for the terrain.

You have a choice of buying a bike with the best components you can get or buying something cheaper and then upgrading it as your wallet permits you to do so. When you upgrade one component at a time, you are able to see what kind of difference the upgrade makes on how the bike performs rather than going all out and upgrading everything and not knowing where the improvements really came from.

As you ride your bike, you will start to notice areas that need improvement over time. For example, let's say your brakes don't stop as well as you like, or they lock up too easily rather than giving you smooth, controlled braking. Then you pull the trigger on a new set of brakes and notice how much better they work and how it has improved your riding. This is when upgrading your bike becomes fun, and you will then look forward to the next component that can be improved upon.

Best Bang for the Buck

There are many upgrades you can make to your mountain bike, and some are better than others, especially when it comes to cost vs. improvement. I will be going over several components that are commonly upgraded in the upcoming sections, but for now I will go over the ones that I think offer the greatest improvement for the money spent, and then you can read about the details when you get to that section.

Going tubeless with your tires is a great upgrade and is very inexpensive. This only requires that you purchase some new valve stems and some sealant, and you are ready to go. Most mountain bike tires are tubeless-ready, meaning that they can run with a standard inner tube inside or without one.

Handlebar upgrades are another one of my favorites. Changing the length or rise of your handlebars can make a huge difference in how your bike performs. This upgrade is also on the cheap side, especially if you are sticking with aluminum handlebars. (Carbon is the better choice in my opinion, though.)

Although I don't have a section on seat upgrades (often called saddles, by the way), I feel that this is a great upgrade as well. If you are going on long rides and have a seat that is not right for you, then you will be asking for a painful day. Unfortunately, this is not the kind of thing that you can buy without doing some homework. There are many types of seats of all different shapes and sizes, and obviously not everyone is the same when it comes to what works for them.

Shock\Fork

Upgrading your suspension can be very expensive, but it does produce some great results. Most factory suspension is geared around everyday users and tuned to try and satisfy the most amount of people. This is great for the bike manufacturers, but it might not be so great for you.

Before you decide to replace your shock or fork, you might want to consider having it tuned to your weight and riding style. Most bike shops can service your shock and fork, but having it tuned is best left to a company that specializes in that sort of thing (like PUSH Industries in Colorado). You can send in your shock or fork and have them rebuild it and tune it to your specifications. You will be amazed at how much better it performs afterward. Just be sure to ask them if they service your particular model. There are other companies out there that do the same type of service.

If you want to get an overall better shock or fork rather than tune what you have, then there are options to replace yours with a better performing model. The key here is to make sure you figure out what will fit on your bike without changing its geometry too much or making it handle worse. Forks can cost over $1,000 for something nice, and shocks can run you $400 and more.

Things to look for include newer damper technology, thicker stanchions if you are taking on tougher terrain, and more adjustability such as low and high speed compression if your current model doesn't have those settings. It's a good idea to do some serious research and maybe even hit up some bike forums to see what others think who use the same suspension components you are thinking about upgrading to.

Wheels

You might not think that your wheels will make a difference in how your bike performs, but they actually do. There are a lot of variables in wheel design that determine how they perform, and different wheels will perform better in different situations.

First, let's go into aluminum vs. carbon fiber wheels, since that has been a debate for some time. Of course, carbon wheels are going to be more expensive and lighter than aluminum wheels, but they are also more rigid for more control. When I got my first set of carbon wheels, I didn't really notice the difference in climbing but did notice the difference going downhill because the bike felt more controlled and maneuverable. Then again, I have friends who think aluminum wheels feel better, so it's hard to say which you will like better. I would recommend trying a similar bike with carbon wheels to see if you notice the difference one way or another. Also keep in mind that carbon wheels are expensive, and you can be looking at around $1,500 and up to get yourself a set.

Wheel width is another reason to upgrade. If you plan on putting some wide tires on your bike yet have skinny wheels, then they will either not fit, or if they do fit they won't fit the way they should. Mountain bike wheels have inner and outer width measurements that are used to determine how wide of a tire you can use. Plus, when you have wider wheels, it will affect how much the tire bulges out. So, if you put a 2.4" tire on a thin wheel and a wide wheel, the tire will actually look bigger on the wider wheel because of the wheel width. Wheels have been getting wider and wider lately, with 28mm becoming a more common factory wheel width.

Hubs and spokes are another reason to upgrade. Sure, you can replace the hubs and spokes on your current wheels, but in order to do that, you will most likely need to pay someone to do the work since it's not something just anyone can do. Plus, the hubs tend to be the most expensive part of the wheel if you get the good stuff, so you might as well just replace the entire wheel. Spoke layout and type can affect the wheel's weight and strength, and wheel companies will make specific types of wheels for cross country, Enduro, and downhill riders.

Tubeless Tires

If you have ridden a mountain bike (or any other type of bike, for that matter), I'm sure you have had a flat tire at some point or another. Fixing a flat is, for the most part, an easy fix, but if you don't have a tube or the right tools, it may ruin your day when you have to walk home. Some flats are easier to fix than others depending on the tire type, whether it's the front or rear tire, and whether or not you know how to replace an inner tube.

What would you say if you didn't have to replace inner tubes anymore and didn't even have to have them inside your tire? Sounds pretty nice, doesn't it? Well, if you have the right kind of tire and the right kind of rim, then this is definitely a possibility for you. Running tubeless is starting to become more popular as more tubeless tires hit the market and as many higher end bikes are coming with tubeless-ready rims and tires.

Using tubes is the standard way to go and is what people have been doing for years. Most bikes come with tubes installed even if they have tubeless-ready tires on them from the factory. The inner tube itself goes between the rim and the tire, providing the inflation the tire needs to work. You can put various amounts of air pressure in the tube to adjust to the trail and your riding style. The higher the pressure, the less likely you are to get pinch flats, but at the same time there is less tire making contact with the ground, and you may find yourself bouncing around more off of rocks and not cornering as well.

Then there is the other side of the spectrum, which is tubeless tires. Sealant is used to make sure no air escapes the tire once you inflate it since there is no tube to hold the air in. Then when you run over something that pokes a hole in the tire, the sealant will fill the hole and seal it up. This will only work for holes of a certain size and whether or not your sealant has dried up or not. Many times you will run over something and the tire will seal itself without you even knowing. When you have a bigger hole you need to turn the wheel so the hole is closest to the ground, allowing the sealant to settle over it and hopefully stop the leak. However, if you put a big gash in the tire, especially on the sidewall, there is a good chance it won't seal it. The sealant will have to be replaced every four months or so depending on the brand and how much you use.

Special valve stems are also required on tubeless tires. Normally the valve stem is part of the inner tube, but when going tubeless you need to mount the valve in the wheel itself and make sure it's airtight. Many of these valve stems will have removable cores, allowing you to add more sealant through the valve stem rather than having to unseat the tire from the wheel.

If your wheels are not tubeless-ready, then you will need to tape them to cover up the spoke holes so no air gets out. There is special tape you can buy that is made for this purpose, and it's fairly easy to apply. Just make sure to get the right width for your wheel or else it won't fit right.

Some people don't notice a real difference between tubeless-ready tires and tubed tires, especially if you run the same air pressure you did while using inner tubes. Tubeless tires are usually always used with downhill riders and more extreme styles of riding where you need the extra performance you get from lower tire pressures. I like running tubeless for the same reason. I find that lower tire pressure allows you to grip better on turns and makes the bike more stable on rocky terrain.

The decision to go tube vs. tubeless should be based on your riding style, the terrain you are riding on, and what type of bike you are riding. Just because you don't like changing tubes doesn't make for a good enough reason to switch to tubeless! You must also be willing to put in the extra work and expense required to get your bike running tubeless, and if you don't like it, then you will have to do the work to switch it back, so keep that in mind. Here are some pros and cons for each:

Inner tube pros

- No extra setup required.
- Easy to fix a flat.
- Cheap to run if you don't get a lot of flats.
- Don't need special tires or wheels.

Tubeless pros

- No tube to replace.
- You can run lower tire pressure for a better grip without pinch flats.
- Running over thorns generally won't flatten the tire.
- Possible lower rolling resistance.

Inner tube cons

- Have to run higher pressure to avoid pinch flats.
- Running over a thorn most likely means you will have to replace the tube.
- Gets pricey if you get a lot of flats.
- Not as much tire contacting the trail thanks to higher pressures.
- Possible higher rolling resistance.

Tubeless cons

- More expensive to set up.
- May require special tires and wheels.
- If you put a hole\rip in your tire it will not hold air.
- You still need to carry a tube for backup.

Brakes

Having well performing brakes is important as you start to push yourself to the limit more and more during your rides. When things are getting rough and you are flying down the trail, you need to be able to stop in a reasonable amount of time and also stop in a controlled fashion.

Even though most mountain bike brakes look similar on the outside, it doesn't mean they are the same on the inside. There are a lot of variables as to how brakes work, and you should pay attention to their specifications when looking for a new braking system.

I mentioned mechanical and hydraulic brakes in Chapter 6, but you really want to stick with hydraulic for performance reasons. Mechanical disk brakes are usually used on cheaper bikes and might eventually fade away. Hydraulic brakes generally offer more stopping power and improved modulation. Modulation describes how much fine control you have when applying braking power when you pull your brake levers. If you have zero modulation, that means that the brakes are simply off or all the way on. Modulation lets you apply braking force as you see fit, kind of like how your car does.

You will find brake calipers that come with either two pistons or four pistons based on how much braking power you need. The pistons are what push the brake pads into the rotors to make you stop. Many people are fine with just two piston brakes, but if you are doing Enduro or downhill riding, then you will probably want four piston brakes to give you that extra stopping power.

Brake rotors also make a difference in how well your bike will stop. Better rotors are made from two separate pieces to facilitate cooling. Some brake pads even come with fins on them to help keep things cooler.

Some people say that the vent hole patterns in rotors make a difference in cooling and performance, but it's really more of a design thing. It may affect how noisy the brakes can be, though.

There are different size rotors for bikes, and the larger rotors have more surface area for better stopping power. Just be sure that your bike can take a larger rotor before making this upgrade. You might be able to put washers under the caliper bolts to give you the clearance or get an adapter bracket.

Handlebars\Stem

I have already discussed handlebars and how the width, rise, and angles will affect how they feel on your bike, but if you think you need to change things out, then this is an upgrade that you should like. Before swapping out your handlebars, try loosening the bolts that connect them to the stem and rotate them in or out to see if that makes things feel better. If so, you can avoid the cost of having to buy new ones.

Handlebars come in aluminum and carbon fiber, just like almost everything else, and of course the carbon fiber bars will be lighter and more expensive. They will also offer more rigidity than aluminum bars and give you a more solid feel while on the trail. Then again, some people prefer aluminum bars over carbon, so it's one of those things you will have to figure out by trying it out.

Adding just a slightly wider handlebar can make a huge difference in how your bike feels and how it performs. As I mentioned earlier, I prefer a 780-800mm wide handlebar, but you might want to start at 760mm if you don't think you want to go that wide. Then again, if you get wider bars, you can usually cut them down to the size you want, unlike narrow bars which obviously you can't make wider. The latest craze is to have thicker handlebars, which will help stiffen things up. I have done this and noticed a slight difference, but nothing too drastic. A nice set of carbon handlebars will cost around $150.

If your handlebars are too low and you don't have any room to add more spacers to bring the bar height up, then you can get some handlebars with a rise to them so they will sit higher up. There are many levels of rise that are measured in degrees, such as a twenty degree rise. You can also change the angle of your stem so it is pointing up rather than level.

Speaking of the stem, this is another upgrade you can do if you want to go shorter or longer based on your needs. A shorter stem will give you more control when going downhill while a longer stem is better suited for climbing and cross country riding.

Stems are relatively inexpensive, so you might want to have more than one so you can try out a longer one and a shorter one and see what works best for you. You might end up with something right in the middle.

Dropper Seatpost
Most decent new mountain bikes will come with a dropper seatpost that allows you to raise and lower the height of the seat as needed while riding. Before these were invented, you would have to constantly stop to manually raise and lower your seat as needed or just ride with it in one position no matter if you were going up or down. As I mentioned before, you want your seat all the way up when climbing, and all the way down when going down something steep or fast. You will also find that having it somewhere in the middle works out for certain situations.

Not all dropper seatposts are the same, and some brands work better than others. You may run into issues where the seat won't stay down or won't go up, and that is not fun when you're out on the trail. These seatposts do require periodic maintenance, but for the most part, they should work trouble free for a long time.

When shopping for a dropper post, be sure to read reviews and talk to people to see how they like the brand they have. Then you will need to determine what size to get in regard to how high it rises and the seatpost diameter on your bike. There are only a couple of sizes to worry about, so it shouldn't be too hard to figure out what diameter you need.

If you are six feet or taller, I would recommend a 150mm dropper or maybe even a 170mm. 125mm is about as short as they go, so if you are on the shorter side, then your choice has been made for you. I am a big fan of the Fox Transfer seatpost myself because it works like a charm and I have had no issues with the two that I have owned. (And no, I don't work for Fox!) A nice dropper seatpost will cost around $200-$400.

Drivetrain

Even though drivetrain upgrades can be on the expensive side, I think they are worth it because if you have a cheap or poorly performing drivetrain, then you will not be having fun out on the trails. There are various components of the drivetrain that can be replaced, or you can go all out and replace the entire thing (budget permitting).

Then again, if your bike came with a nice drivetrain setup, then you are lucky and can save yourself some money and maybe just replace the parts that can use the upgrade such as getting a lighter cassette or carbon fiber cranks to take some weight off of the bike.

You usually want to replace the pieces that work together (like the shifter and derailleur) at once and stick with the same brand or same series. For example, SRAM makes its twelve speed Eagle set that comes with the entire drivetrain, and all the components are designed to work together with each other. If you start mismatching brands and models, things might not work out so smoothly.

I mentioned replacing the cranks with carbon fiber ones. This is a great upgrade because it can save you a decent amount of weight, and weight is the enemy of mountain bikers. Just make sure you get the type that works with your frame and keep the crank arm length the same as the cranks you are replacing unless you have a good reason to go shorter or longer. A set of carbon cranks will set you back around $200-$300.

The derailleur will control how smoothly the bike shifts, so be sure not to go cheap on this component. There are many models at many price ranges, and yes, there are even ones with carbon fiber cages to save weight. A nice derailleur will also set you back around $200-$300.

What's Next

Now that you have a better understanding of what to look for in a mountain bike and how all the basic components work together to get you down the trail, you can begin your search for the perfect bike. Well, I should say the perfect bike for your budget!

Just remember not to start with anything super expensive unless you are sure that you are going to stick with it. Once the bike leaves the bike shop, it depreciates in value, just like a new car would. Plus, you don't want to be stuck trying to sell a used bike after realizing you don't want to ride it.

If you want to get some training to get a head start on your riding career then you can take a seminar or class on riding and learn from instructors who have been riding for years. Check with your local bike shop or bike park to see if you can find any classes that are available in your area.

I had mentioned *pinkbike.com* in this book, and it's a great resource to get information about bikes in general, as well as learn how they work and how to work on them yourself. They are also a great resource for riding tips, and if you join the site you will have access to the forum to ask questions of your fellow riders. And don't forget about *trailforks.com* to find information about local trails, and also my site, *mtbcommunity.com*, for additional information on bike gear and informative blog posts.

About the Author

Jim Bernstein has been riding mountain bikes for over 20 years and has ridden various locations around the country. He enjoys challenging trails and testing his skills whenever possible. Jim also enjoys working on bikes and helping others with their own bikes when he can. He enjoys riding as many new trails as he can, and is always looking for the next adventure.

Jim started a website dedicated to mountain biking in his community and in other locations. The site is called ***mtbcommunity.com*** and has been around for many years. With this site, he and his riding group are able to map out trails as well as offer reviews, photos, and videos of these trails. The site also offers product reviews on a variety of mountain bike accessories and components, plus there is a blog that is updated on a regular basis that offers helpful tips and advice for its readers.

Made in the USA
Las Vegas, NV
16 December 2023

82972870R00090